STELLA STANDARD'S
SOUP BOOK

Stella Standard's
SOUP BOOK

BY STELLA STANDARD

Taplinger Publishing Company / New York

First Edition
Published in the United States in 1978 by
TAPLINGER PUBLISHING CO., INC.
New York, New York

Copyright © 1978 by Stella Standard

Library of Congress Cataloging in Publication Data
Standard, Stella.
    Stella Standard's soup book.

    Includes index.
    1. Soups. I. Title. II. Title: Soup book.
TX757.S73   1978   641.8′13   78-58292
ISBN 0-8008-7381-5

Designed by Manuel Weinstein

To the memory of
ANDRE L. SIMON

Contents

Introduction

Until the seventh century, people made some sort of brew in huge cauldrons that received everything available: cereals, vegetables, game, if any, and bread. As civilization proceeded, methods of food production developed and eating habits changed, but the soup habit persisted, and became world-wide, and today soup is properly acknowledged as basic, nutritious, and therefore indispensable to man's diet.

Grimod de la Reynière and Brillat-Savarin, two oft-quoted gourmets, were born in the 1750's and were friends and jurists who devoted much of their lives to the delights of the table. De la Reynière wrote a *Manuel des Amphitryons* and an *Almanac des Gourmands;* Brillat-Savarin wrote the well-known *Physiology of Taste.* Brillat-Savarin attended monthly dinners at the home of de la Reynière, where serious and devoted diners passed judgment on dishes sent in by tradesmen interested in publicity. Both wrote philosophical treatises on the culinary arts, and what they had to say is as pertinent today as it was then. De la Reynière wrote that soup was to a dinner what a portico or peristyle was to a building; that is to say, it sets the tone of the whole banquet in the same way the overture announces the subject of the opera.

Brillat-Savarin was more explicit, distinguishing between the two basic soups, bouillon and potage. "We apply the phrase pot-au-feu to a piece of beef boiled in slightly salted water, with the object of extracting its soluble parts. The liquid which is left at the end of the operation is called bouillon. The residue of meat, when the soluble part of the meat has been extracted, we call bouilli. . . .

"To make good bouillon, it is essential that the water come to a boil slowly to prevent the albumen from coagulating inside the meat before extraction. It should boil quite gently so that the components which successively dissolve may easily and thoroughly commingle. Vegetables were added to bring out the flavor, and bread or dough to make it more nutritious. With these additions, bouillon became potage. Potage is a light, wholesome, and nutritious form of food which agrees with everyone; it stimulates the receptive and digestive faculties of the stomach. It is said that nowhere can such good potage be obtained as in France; and my own travels have proved the justice of the saying. And, indeed, it is what might be expected; for potage is the basis for the French national diet, and the experience of centuries has inevitably brought it to perfection.''

Bread was used to thicken soup and was dipped into the soup to soften and use up dry bread; two habits retained to this day. Soup is the earliest food custom, and in both China and France, soup is still the national dish; congee in China, potage in France. All western soups are French in origin.

Soup in France is taken very seriously in the home; in some it is served twice a day. If soup is made with care, it is made with stock. There is an erroneous idea outside the country that the soup kettle never ceases to bubble, and that anything and everything is thrown into it. For instance, had a pot of soup been started during the Crimean War as a continuous operation it would still be there on the back of the stove, bubbling merrily. Nothing could be further from the truth. Everything that goes into the soup pot is perfect food, not something unsuitable for anything else. Meat, poultry, and bones go with the appropriate vegetables into the soup. And after two or three days that pot will have been consumed, and a new pot-au-feu is begun with fresh utensils and fresh food. Different provinces have their own long-time favorites, using the available vegetables, meat, and game. This book contains many of these regional soups, including recipes from several three-star restaurants, as well as some others that deserve this distinction.

*   *   *

No matter how small the family, if soup is a daily habit there can never be too much. Soup stock can be used in countless ways. There is nothing better or more convenient for lunch or to begin a dinner for two or for a party of ten. It is the ideal first course.

As an opening course, soup serves admirably to separate the aperitif from the wine to be served with the fish or meat. The palate is then ready for a complete change. On occasion, you might want to serve a wine with the soup. A dry Amontillado sherry would go well with shrimp bisque, a dry fino sherry with lobster bisque, or champagne as suggested by Paul Genin of Chez Pauline. A light Moselle would go well with mushroom soup; a dry white wine with mussel soup. Serve Montilla sherry or Madeira with oxtail soup. Burgundy or claret goes with game soup. Oyster soup calls for Chablis, onion soup a white Burgundy. If Madeira is served as an aperitif, it may be continued with turtle soup.

To be a good soup maker you must have certain equipment. One of the most important items is a 14-quart soup kettle. When meat, chicken, and vegetables are cooked together, there should be no crowding. For smaller quantities, 2-, 4-, and 6-quart pots are most useful. A fish cooker with a rack is quite necessary for draining out fish so that it does not break. There are wonderful fish soups that specify serving whole fish or fillets either in the soup or on the side. I find a 4-quart pressure cooker invaluable for retaining the flavors and nutrients of green vegetables that go into soups. The electric blender is a real must. It purées in a matter of seconds to make watery soups velvety in texture. It purées leftover vegetables with milk or broth to make delicious soups. A blender saves enough food to pay for itself in a matter of months. The meat grinder is an old standby, as are sieves from coarse to fine. Measuring cups and spoons and rubber spatulas (the great food saver) of course we all have.

Since the French are the master soup makers we have naturally taken over some of their terms.

Bisque: a rich thick soup, most often made of fish or seafood.
Bouillon, broth, consommé: thin, clear soup, made by straining meat or poultry stock (see Stock). Various seasonings may be added. The terms are used interchangeably in recipes.

Chowder: usually a soup made of fish or seafood and vegetables but also used for corn chowder which does not contain fish.

Stock: foundation for soups, made of bones, meat, poultry, or game, and vegetables. Brown stock (*fonds brun*) usually contains beef; the meat and bones are browned before the stock is made. White stock (*fonds blanc*) is made with veal; poultry stock (*fonds de vollaile*) with chicken; the ingredients for both are put into the soup kettle without previous browning. Fish stock (*fumet*) is made with fish and fish trimmings (skin, bones, head) and is cooked a much shorter time than are meat or poultry stocks.

Not every kitchen has stock on hand at all times. Meat glaze and beef and chicken soup concentrates are especially useful and should always be on the pantry shelf. Good meat and bones should always be saved for stock. Stock instead of water in making soups is the difference between something with flavor and nourishment and something without. For instance, always make onion or mushroom soups with stock and you will have something very fine. Canned vegetable juice and carrot juice may be used as part of the liquid in a large pot of vegetable soup. Keep cans of both on hand.

Since no dish is better than its ingredients, only the best should go into soup. Wine is a great addition for some soups. I specify Madeira very often, since some cooks, of which I am one, much prefer it to sherry. However, a good sherry may be used when Madeira is not available. The French, more often than not, use sherry only when making Spanish dishes.

Brillat-Savarin said the secret of good soup is "long, slow cooking." I have said "simmer gently" hundreds of times—I don't know a better way of putting it. Soup is nourishing for the rich and the poor, the old and the young, the sick and the well. The steaming kettle perfumes the house and whets the appetite. It yields the very essence of the good things that go into it.

Stocks, Meat, and Poultry Soups

Cooking Bones and Meats for Soup

There are a few general rules for cooking bones and meats for soup. Put the meat and bones in cold water and bring slowly to a simmer. This method will extract the gelatin. Sometimes cold meat stock is used, instead of water. Beginning the cooking in cold liquid extracts the maximum of food value, proteins, and gelatin from the meat and bones. For clear stock add salt sparingly at the beginning and correct the seasoning at the finish. When the soup meat is to be served apart from the soup, put it into boiling water or stock to seal in the juices. In making brown stock for rich soups and sauces, put the meat, bones, and whole onions in a very hot oven and roast to a rich brown, then put them in liquid and bring to a simmer. Skim all stocks when they come to a simmer to remove all scum. Specific instructions are given in each recipe.

Brown Stock *(Fonds Brun)*

3 pounds round, rump, or shin of
  beef, cubed
2 pounds bones
1 veal knuckle, split
1 whole onion, unpeeled
2 onions, sliced
2 carrots, sliced
2 whole cloves
1 teaspoon thyme
2 bay leaves
2 cloves garlic, halved

2 stalks celery, sliced
2 sprigs parsley
1 cup red wine
1 cup of tomato purée
3½ quarts hot water
Salt and pepper

FOR CLARIFYING

2 half-beaten egg whites
3 tablespoons ground raw beef
3 tablespoons chopped parsley

Roast the meat, bones, knuckle, and whole onion in a dripping pan 25 or 30 minutes in a 450° oven, turning them halfway through the roasting. Put all into a large soup kettle. Rinse out the pan with hot water and add to the kettle. Add the rest of the ingredients except the salt and pepper. Cover, bring to the simmer, and skim. Cook, covered, very slowly 3½ hours, adding salt and pepper after 2 hours. If you wish to obtain a clear stock, strain without pressing the vegetables against the sieve, chill, and remove the cake of fat. Every bit of fat must be removed if the stock is to be clarified. If a sparkling gelatin is desired, clarify by bringing the stock to the simmer; stir in the half-beaten egg whites, beef, and parsley. Simmer 20 minutes. Line a sieve with a damp cloth and strain the stock. The veal knuckle should provide enough gelatin to obtain an aspic, but if the stock doesn't jell, measure the liquid and for each pint, soak 2 teaspoons of gelatin in a little cold water or lemon juice and melt in a little hot stock. Add to the rest of the stock and chill. *Makes about 4 quarts*

White Stock *(Fonds Blanc)*

3 pounds neck and shoulder of veal
1½ pounds veal bone
1 veal knuckle, split
2 carrots, diced
2 onions, diced
1 whole onion stuck with 3 cloves
3½ quarts water

3 bay leaves
3 stalks celery, sliced
3 springs parsley
1 teaspoon basil
1 teaspoon thyme
1 cup of dry white wine
Salt and pepper

Put all the ingredients except the salt and pepper in a large soup kettle. Bring to the simmer and skim until all the scum is removed. Cover and simmer 3½ hours; after 2 hours add the salt and pepper. Strain the soup and then strain again through a sieve lined with a damp cloth. This will jell. If you want a sparkling aspic, see Brown Stock in the index for the method of clarifying. This is the base for many soups. *Makes about 3½ quarts*

Poultry Stock *(Fonds de Volaille)*

3 pounds chicken soup parts
   (wings, backs, necks, giblets)
1 veal knuckle, split
2 carrots, sliced
2 good-sized onions, sliced
1 whole onion stuck with 3 cloves
2 bay leaves
3 stalks celery, sliced

3 sprigs parsley
1 teaspoon basil
1 teaspoon thyme
1 cup dry white wine
2 teaspoons chicken soup
   concentrate
3½ quarts water
Salt and pepper

In a large kettle put all the ingredients except the salt and pepper; this is added after the soup has cooked 1½ hours. Cover, bring gently to the simmer, and cook 2½ hours. If you want a clear soup or an aspic, strain the soup without pressing the vegetables against the sieve. See Brown Stock in the index for clarifying. The chicken parts and veal knuckle provide enough bones to obtain an aspic without adding commercial gelatin. This is the base for many soups: mushroom, noodle, potato, bean, leek and so on. *Makes about 3½ quarts*

Beef Bouillon

2 pounds beef knuckle and marrow bones
2 pounds chopped beef
1 whole chicken
2 cups chopped carrots
2 cups chopped celery
3 sprigs parsley
1 white turnip, peeled and sliced
1 parsnip, sliced
2 bay leaves

1 can vegetable juice
1 can carrot juice
2 cups red wine
1 teaspoon basil
1 teaspoon thyme
2 whole cloves
2 half-beaten egg whites (for clarifying)
Salt and pepper

Have the beef knuckle cracked. Put all the ingredients except the egg whites and salt and pepper in a 14-quart kettle. Add cold water to just cover. Cover the kettle and bring slowly to the boil and skim until all scum is removed. After 1 hour's cooking, remove the chicken, which may be served hot, used cold in salad, or creamed. Continue simmering gently for 3 hours, adding a little hot water only if necessary, since the bouillon must be of good flavor. When the bouillon is done, remove the bones and strain. For a clear soup, do not press the vegetables against the sieve. Let the soup cool, chill it, and then remove the cake of fat from the top. Every bit of fat must be removed if it is to be clarified. Season the soup with salt and pepper, bring to the simmer with the half-beaten egg whites, and cook 15 minutes. Line a sieve with a damp cloth and strain the soup; it will be clear. Chill thoroughly, and store in screw-topped glass jars. This is the base of many sauces and for a variety of soups: mushroom, onion, bean and so on. If it is served as clear bouillon, Madeira may be added and croutons and cheese passed. *Makes about 4 quarts*

Chicken Broth

3 pounds chicken soup parts
  (wings, backs, necks, giblets)
1 knuckle of veal, split
Marrow bones
1½ cups sliced celery and leaves
1½ cups chopped onions
2 carrots, chopped
1 parsnip, sliced
1 teaspoon thyme

1 teaspoon basil
1 teaspoon chervil
2 whole cloves
1 cup dry white wine
Water to cover
3 teaspoons chicken soup
  concentrate mixed with boiling
  water
Salt and pepper

Put all the ingredients except the soup concentrate, salt, and pepper in a soup kettle. Mix the soup concentrate with a little boiling water and add it. Cover and simmer gently 2 hours, adding the salt and pepper after 45 minutes. (If you wish, cook a small chicken or chicken breasts, legs, or thighs in the soup 45 minutes to an hour, remove, and serve separately.) Strain the soup. This is a fine soup as is, or a base for many other soups: noodle, mushroom, vichyssoise, onion, potato, leek, and so on. This can be used to make an aspic that is delightful in summer topped with minced green onions and a teaspoon of caviar. *Makes about 3 quarts*

Consommé Double

1 oxtail, cut in pieces
1 pound ground lean rump of beef
2 quarts hot rich beef stock
1 onion stuck with 3 cloves
½ cup Madeira

GARNISH

Fresh minced tarragon or chervil
12 slices of poached marrow

This is one of the most important soups in French cuisine. Put the oxtail and beef in a heavy frying pan and roast it 12 minutes in a preheated 500° oven. Put the meats in a soup kettle with the hot beef stock and the onion, cover, and simmer gently 2 hours. Strain through a damp cloth, cool, and strain through a cloth again. Reheat before serving; then add the Madeira. Roll the slices of marrow in the minced herb, put 2 slices in each hot soup cup, and pour in the consommé. *Serves 6*

Bouillon with Madeira

6 cups beef, veal, or chicken broth
²/₃ cup Madeira
¼ teaspoon cinnamon
⅛ teaspoon powdered clove
A few grinds of a whole nutmeg
2 egg yolks

1 tablespoon light brown sugar

GARNISH

Croutons fried in butter and shaken
  with 2 tablespoons powdered
  sugar

Boil up the broth with the wine and spices. Beat the egg yolks with the sugar until thick and whisk into the hot bouillon. Add a few croutons to the top of each serving. Beef bouillon is especially good for this. *Serves 6*

Consommé with Veal Quenelles

3 tablespoons butter, melted
2 tablespoons flour
6½ cups hot rich veal, chicken, or
  beef broth

3 tablespoons fresh herbs:
Minced tarragon, chives, parsley, or
  chervil
30 veal quenelles (see index)

In the bottom of a good-sized pot, make a roux of the melted butter and flour, blending until smooth. Cook over low heat until it colors ivory. Blend with a little hot broth and when smooth add the rest of the broth and the herbs. Bring to a simmer. Cook the quenelles in the broth 6 or 7 minutes, covered. Drain the quenelles, put 5 into each hot soup plate and divide the consommé over them. *Serves 6*

Tagliarini al Consommé *(Broth with Thin Noodles)*

4 to 6 ounces finest egg noodles
8 cups rich beef, veal, or chicken
  consommé

GARNISH

Grated Parmesan or Gruyère cheese

Simmer the noodles gently in the consommé until tender, or cook them separately in salted boiling water. Drain and divide into hot soup plates and pour boiling consommé over them. Pass a bowl of cheese. This soup is very popular in Italy, where it is known as *Tagliarini in Brodo*. *Serves 8*

Oxtail Soup

3 pounds oxtails
1 clove garlic, crushed
1 cup chopped onions
1 cup chopped carrots
1 white turnip, peeled and diced

8 cups beef bouillon
Salt and pepper
1 cup dry white wine
Madeira

Wash the oxtails and cut them in 4-inch lengths. Put them in a pot with all the other ingredients except the wines. (If bouillon is not available, use 8 cups of water and 3 teaspoons beef glaze or beef soup concentrate.) Bring to the simmer and skim. Cover and cook slowly 1½ hours. Remove the oxtails and purée the soup in the blender. Put the oxtails in a pan, pour in the white wine, cover, and simmer 10 minutes. Remove the oxtails. Take off all the meat from the bones and add it, with the wine, to the soup. Put 1 tablespoon of Madeira in each soup plate and add the boiling soup. *Serves 6 to 8*

Veal and Chicken Broth

1 veal shank, split
1 veal knuckle, split
1 cup diced onions
1 cup diced carrots
1 white turnip, peeled and diced
1 leek, sliced
1 cup sliced celery and leaves
1 teaspoon meat glaze
2 quarts water

2 teaspoons chicken soup
   concentrate
6 to 8 chicken pieces: legs, thighs, or
   half-breasts
Salt and pepper
1/3 cup tomato purée
1/3 cup vermicelli
1 cup heavy cream

Put the ingredients up to and including the concentrate into the soup kettle. Cover and simmer gently 2 hours. Add one chicken piece for each serving, salt and pepper to taste, and the tomato purée. Simmer gently 30 minutes or until the chicken is tender. Remove all the meats and keep them warm. Strain the soup. Add the vermicelli and simmer 15 minutes, then add the cream. Serve the soup first and serve the meats accompanied with a green vegetable or a potato dish, as a separate course. *Serves 6 to 8*

Beef and Oxtail Soup

2 pounds rump, chuck, or brisket of
  beef, cubed
1 oxtail, cut in 5 pieces
2 veal shin bones with meat and
  marrow
1 onion, quartered
1 whole onion stuck with 3 cloves
1 cup chopped onions
1 cup chopped carrots
¾ cup tomato purée
1 large leek, sliced
½ cup sliced celery

3 tablespoons minced parsley
1 cup red wine
3 white turnips, peeled and diced
1 teaspoon thyme
3 bay leaves
1 teaspoon basil
1 teaspoon marjoram
2 cloves garlic, crushed
3 quarts boiling water
Salt and pepper
2 tablespoons cornstarch
⅔ cup Madeira or sherry

Wash the meat and bones and dry with paper towels. Put them and the quartered onion in a dripping pan and roast at 450° 25 to 30 minutes, turning once. This browning will enhance the flavor of the soup. Put the meat, bones, and onion with the other ingredients (except the salt, pepper, cornstarch, and wine) in a large soup kettle. If any meat or glaze has stuck to the dripping pan, scrape the pan and rinse with boiling water, adding this to the kettle. Cover and simmer gently 3 hours, adding salt and pepper after 1½ hours. Remove the meat and bones and purée the soup in a blender or mash the vegetables through a sieve. The blender gives a very smooth texture. Extract the marrow from the bones, mix it with the cornstarch and wine and blend smooth in a small bowl. Dilute with a little of the soup, then add to the rest of the soup. Bring to the boil, and serve. The meats may be served to the family as a separate course with creamed horseradish sauce and mashed potatoes. *Serves 10*

Cervelle Velouté *(Brain Soup Velouté)*

1 pair calf's brains
½ cup finely chopped onions
¼ cup butter
1 clove garlic, peeled
Salt and pepper
4 cups hot veal or chicken broth
2 egg yolks

½ cup heavy cream

GARNISHES

Croutons fried in butter
Veal quenelles (see index)
Chopped pistachio nuts

Soak the brains in cold salted water 1 hour; then take them out and remove all the membranes. Dry the brains on a clean cloth and cut them in small pieces. Sauté the onions in the butter until they soften, then stir in the brains, garlic, salt, and pepper. Cover and cook gently 10 minutes. Remove the garlic and purée the contents of the pan in a blender with some of the broth, then add the rest of the broth. Scald the cream and stir in the egg yolks. When ready to serve, whisk the cream mixture into the hot soup. Garnish, if you wish, with croutons, tiny veal quenelles, or nuts. This is an elegant smooth soup. *Serves 6*

Velouté au Ris de Veau *(Sweetbread and Pea Soup)*

1 sweetbread	3 tablespoons butter
½ cup dry white wine	¾ cup heavy cream
6 cups veal or chicken broth	2 egg yolks
1 pound fresh peas	
1 teaspoon basil	GARNISH
Salt and pepper	3 tablespoons minced chives

Soak the sweetbread in cold salted water 1 hour; then take it out and remove all the membranes. Cut the sweetbread in small segments and put in a heavy pot with the wine and ½ cup of the broth. Cover and simmer gently 15 minutes. Remove half of the sweetbread and reserve. Purée the rest of the sweetbread and the liquid with some of the broth in the blender until creamy and smooth and add to the pot with the rest of the broth. Rinse the blender with some of the broth. Cook the fresh peas with the basil, salt, and pepper in as little water as possible. Add them to the soup. Sauté the reserved sweetbread in the butter until golden. Do this quickly as the sweetbread should be soft inside. Add to the soup. Scald the cream, stir in the egg yolks, then whisk into the hot soup. Reheat without boiling. Sprinkle the top of each plate of soup with chives. *Serves 8*

Game Soup

Carcass and meat of roast game bird	Leftover dressing and gravy, or ½
1 cup chopped onions	cup cooked rice
1 cup chopped carrots	6 cups chicken or beef bouillon
½ cup sliced celery and leaves	¼ cup heavy cream
2 leeks, sliced	⅓ cup good port wine
Bouquet garni: thyme, parsley, chervil	

Pound the carcass and put it in the bottom of a soup kettle. Add all the ingredients except the cream and wine. (If bouillon is not at hand, use 6 cups of water and 2 tablespoons each chicken and beef soup concentrate.) Cover and simmer gently 1 hour. Remove all the bones, take off any meat clinging to them, and purée it with the rest of the soup. Season with salt and pepper if needed. Bring to the boil and add the cream and wine. Serve in soup cups. Without the cream this broth can be used as the base for an excellent mushroom soup (see index). *Serves 6*

Potage de Volaille Suprème *(Supreme of Chicken Soup)*

1 2-pound whole chicken or chicken
  parts
6 cups rich chicken consommé
1/3 cup Patna rice, washed
1/4 cup lightly browned almonds
1/3 cup Madeira

1 cup heavy cream
2 egg yolks

GARNISH

1/4 cup sliced browned almonds

If the whole chicken is used, cut it in serving pieces. Put the chicken pieces in a heavy pot. Add the consommé and the rice. Cover and bring to a simmer so slowly that it takes 20 minutes. Cook 40 minutes altogether. Remove the chicken, take the meat off the bones, and purée 1 cup of the meat with the soup and rice to a creamy texture. Pulverize the almonds in the blender and add them and the Madeira. When ready to serve, reheat the soup. Scald the cream, stir it into the egg yolks, and whisk into the soup. Do not boil again. Scatter a few sliced, browned almonds over each plate of soup. *Serves 8*

Game Bird Soup

Make this fine soup when you have too few birds to serve. Quail, ducks, squab, guinea hen, pheasant, or a combination may be used.

3 or 4 birds, quartered
3 tablespoons butter
3 tablespoons oil
2 tablespoons brown sugar
1/2 cup chopped onions
1/2 cup chopped carrots
1 parsnip, chopped
1 white turnip, peeled and chopped
1 cup sliced celery
2 teaspoons marjoram
1 teaspoon thyme

1 cup red wine
6 cups chicken broth, or more
Salt and pepper
1 cup heavy cream
2 egg yolks
1/2 cup Madeira or 1 jigger cognac

GARNISH

Chopped parsley
Quartered chestnuts or croutons
  fried in butter (optional)

Melt the butter, add the oil and sugar, and glaze the bird quarters on both sides until golden. Put them into a soup kettle with the vegetables, herbs, red wine, and enough broth to just cover. Cover and simmer gently 1¼ hour or until the meat is very tender. Remove the meat from the bones. Cube enough meat to make 2 cups and reserve. Strain the soup and purée it with the rest of the meat. Add the cubed meat. Season with salt and pepper if necessary. When ready to serve, reheat the soup. Scald the cream, mix it with the egg yolks, and whisk into the soup. Do not let boil. Add the wine or cognac. Serve in soup plates. Sprinkle each serving with a little parsley and add chestnuts or croutons if desired. Serves 8 or more

Potage à la Reine (Chicken and Rice Soup)

2 pounds chicken thighs and breasts
1 cup dry white wine
7 or 8 cups chicken broth
Bouquet garni: tarragon, basil, parsley
1 cup finely chopped onion
1 carrot, sliced

3 tablespoons Patna rice
Salt and pepper
1 cup heavy cream
2 egg yolks

GARNISH

Sliced almonds, lightly browned

Put all the ingredients except the salt, pepper, cream, and egg yolks in a soup kettle. Cover and simmer gently about 45 minutes. Remove the chicken pieces and cut off the meat. Fill 1 cup with small pieces of meat from the breasts, packing it closely, and purée with 2 cups of the soup. Cut the rest of the chicken meat in julienne sticks and reserve. Strain the rest of the soup and add the purée and the julienne sticks. If the soup is too thick add a little more wine. Scald the cream and mix it with the egg yolks. Reheat the soup and add the cream mixture. Do not boil again. Pour the soup into soup plates and sprinkle each with almonds. Serves 8

Giblet Soup

½ to 1 pound chicken hearts
½ to 1 pound chicken gizzards
Chicken soup parts (backs, wings, necks)
2/3 cup chopped onions
2/3 cup chopped carrots
2 stalks celery and leaves, sliced
Bouquet garni: thyme, parsley, chervil
2 quarts water

3 teaspoons chicken soup concentrate
1 cup dry white wine
1 tablespoon grated lemon rind
2 tablespoons minute tapioca

GARNISH

8 chicken livers, sliced
3 tablespoons butter
3 tablespoons chopped parsley

Cut the hearts and gizzards in half and put them in a soup kettle with all the other ingredients except the tapioca. Cover and cook 1¼ hours. Strain the soup. Add the tapioca and simmer 5 minutes. Cook the sliced livers in the butter until browned but still pink inside, sprinkle with parsley, and add to the soup. Add more salt and pepper if the soup needs it. *Serves 6*

Curry Consommé with Fruit

¾ cup tart apple cut in julienne sticks	2 tablespoons curry powder
½ cup Madeira	8 cups beef or chicken consommé
1 cup black cherries, pitted	2 tablespoons chutney
	¼ cup minute tapioca or vermicelli

Put the apple sticks in a bowl and add the Madeira, then the cherries. Cover and marinate 1 hour. Mix the curry powder with 1 cup of the consommé and heat in the top of a double boiler over simmering water 15 minutes. Add the chutney, the 7 remaining cups of consommé, and the tapioca or vermicelli. Cook gently over direct heat for 15 minutes. Add the fruits and Madeira, reheat, and serve. This soup is delicious served cold in summer.

VARIATION: If chicken consommé is used, ½ cup of heavy cream may be added. *Serves 8*

Passatelli alla Romagnola *(Thickened Consommé)*
Sampieri, Bologna

The recipe was given to me by Annida Gennaro, chef of this favorite old-fashioned restaurant on the street of the same name. Annida is one of those busy people who will stop and cook anything you fancy whether it is on the day's menu or not. She is a great cook and a great friend.

2 eggs, beaten	A few grains nutmeg
½ cup fresh breadcrumbs	6 to 8 cups simmering chicken
¾ cup grated Parmesan cheese	consommé
1 tablespoon melted butter	

Combine all the ingredients except the consommé into quite a dense mixture. In Bologna the mixture is pressed through a *stampo apposta*, which looks like a giant garlic press (lacking this a very coarse sieve can be used), into simmering consommé, and cooked 2 minutes. This makes a delicious soup, a specialty of the old Bolognese cuisine. *Serves 6 to 8*

Potage Mimosa *(Creamed Chicken Soup)*

6 cups rich chicken consommé
1/3 cup Madeira or sherry
1/3 cup heavy cream, whipped

1/3 cup sour cream
Salt and freshly ground pepper
Yolks of 3 hard-cooked eggs

Bring the consommé to the boil and add the wine. Mix the whipped cream with the sour cream and season with salt and pepper. Pour the soup into soup plates, put a dollop of the cream mixture on top of each, sieve the egg yolks over the cream, and serve immediately. *Serves 6*

Complete-Meal Soups

Pot-au-Feu

3 or 4 pounds fresh brisket or chuck
6 marrow bones
1 veal knuckle, split
3½ quarts boiling water
1 large onion stuck with 3 cloves
1 cup finely chopped onions
2 leeks, sliced thin
3 stalks celery, finely sliced
2 carrots, finely sliced
¼ cup chopped parsley
1 teaspoon thyme
2 bay leaves

6 whole white onions
6 whole young carrots
6 small white turnips, peeled
6 whole small parsnips
6 whole potatoes, peeled
2 tablespoons salt
Freshly ground pepper

ACCOMPANIMENTS

Salted marrow on crackers or bread
Dijon mustard and pickles

This makes a grand meal. For more than 6, prepare additional whole vegetables. The vegetables are diced and sliced fine because the soup is not strained. If brisket is used, trim off much of its fat so the soup will not be too greasy. Put the meat, bones, and veal knuckle in a soup kettle and pour the boiling water over them. Bring to a simmer and skim well. Add the whole onion, chopped vegetables, and herbs. Cover and simmer 1½ hours, then add salt and pepper. Simmer 1 more hour or until the meat is tender. In a separate pot, bring the whole vegetables to a boil. Drain them, put them on top of the soup, cover, and cook until they are tender, 25 to 30 minutes. Remove them and the meat and bones from the soup. Serve the meat, marrow bones, and whole vegetables on a large hot platter, accompanied by small bowls of soup. Marrow is a great delicacy; it is extracted from the bones and spread on crackers·or bread. Pass mustard or pickles. Red wine is usually served with pot-au-feu. *Serves 6 or more*

Pot-au-Feu Ancien *(Old-Fashioned Pot-au-Feu)*

In some French provinces mutton is used for this, but beef is more traditional.

3 pounds round or plate of beef
1 pound brisket
1½ pounds cracked bones
3½ quarts boiling water
2 whole onions, roasted
2 whole onions, each stuck with 2 cloves
2 tablespoons salt
2 teaspoons freshly ground pepper
1 large carrot, sliced
2 teaspoons each basil, chervil, and thyme
3 stalks celery, sliced

1 cup chopped onions
3 cloves garlic, crushed
6 whole potatoes
6 whole new carrots
6 small white turnips, peeled
6 small parsnips
1 new cabbage, cut in sixths

ACCOMPANIMENTS

Black bread and butter
Dijon mustard
Creamed horseradish
Beaujolais

Roast two onions in a 500° oven until almost black to give a rich flavor to the broth. Wash the meat and bones, put them in a soup kettle and add the boiling water. Bring to a simmer and skim well. Add all the ingredients up to and including the garlic, cover, and simmer 2½ hours. Put the rest of the vegetables in a separate pot with cold water to cover, bring to a boil, drain, and put on top of the soup. Cover and cook 30 more minutes or until vegetables are tender. Serve the broth in bowls, keeping the whole vegetables and the meat warm in the kettle. Then put these on a hot platter and serve with the accompaniments. Store the broth that is left in screwtop glass jars; when it is cold, remove the cake of fat from the tops of the jars. This broth makes a base for a variety of other soups. *Serves 6 to 8*

Petite Marmite

1½ pounds brisket, cubed
2 quarts beef broth, or water and beef soup concentrate
2 whole cloves
1 cup finely chopped onions
½ cup finely chopped carrots
1 white turnip, peeled and diced fine
1 leek, sliced fine
Salt and freshly ground pepper

1 teaspoon chervil
1 teaspoon thyme
1 teaspoon basil
6 chicken legs with thighs
6 marrow bones
3 cups coarsely chopped cabbage

ACCOMPANIMENT

Salted marrow and toast

The dish is named for the earthenware vessel it is cooked in. It is served from the marmite at the table. The soup is not strained, so the vegetables must be diced fine. Put the meat in the marmite with the beef broth, or the water and soup concentrate. (Chicken soup concentrate and a pea-sized lump of beef glaze may also be used.) Add all the other ingredients except the chicken pieces, marrow bones, and cabbage. Cover and cook gently 1½ hours. Add the chicken, marrow bones, and cabbage. Simmer gently 30 minutes. Put a marrow bone and a piece of chicken on each heated plate. Serve the soup in bowls at the same time. Extract the marrow from the bone, salt it a little, and spread it on hot toast as an accompaniment. *Serves 6*

Petite Marmite Henri IV
André L. Simon

This is a small edition of a pot-au-feu—that is, a brew or broth of meat and vegetables. The petite marmite is usually made of boned beef, a small hen, a knuckle of veal, and fowl's giblets, put into the stock pot, covered with water, and allowed to simmer for a long time; the surface fat and scum being carefully skimmed off from time to time. Carrots, onions, turnips, and leeks are boiled at the same time; a bouquet garni is of course *de rigueur*; pepper and salt to taste. The *Henri IV* petite marmite always has a fowl boiled in the pot, whatever else may be missing.

André Simon's *French Cook Book*
(Courtesy Little, Brown & Co., Boston)

Garbure *(Vegetable Soup with Pork)*

This Béarnais soup can be made with game, goose, or meat bones, and a variety of vegetables. We may choose fresh pork butt or a ham end with meat on it.

2 cups dried white or flageolet
   beans
6 cups water
2 or 3 pounds fresh pork butt
Game or poultry bones if available
1½ cups diced carrots
1 large onion, diced
1 large whole onion stuck with 3
   cloves
5 whole cloves garlic
2 quarts hot water
2 or 3 cups shredded cabbage
2 white turnips, peeled and diced

2 leeks, sliced
1 cup finely sliced celery
1 cup fresh lima beans
1 cup sliced green beans
2 large potatoes, diced
2 teaspoons basil
2 teaspoons chervil
2 tablespoons minced fresh herbs
Salt and freshly ground pepper

ACCOMPANIMENTS

Dijon mustard
Horseradish

Wash the dried beans and soak them overnight in the 6 cups of water. Two or more hours before dinner put the beans and their soaking water in a large soup kettle and add the meat, bones, carrots, onions, and garlic. Add 2 quarts of hot water, cover, and simmer gently 1½ hours. Then add all the rest of the vegetables and the seasonings. Simmer gently 30 to 40 minutes more. The water should cover the vegetables, so you may need to add a little more boiling water. Check for salt and pepper. When the meat and vegetables are done, discard the bones (if used), and drain out the meat. Serve the soup in bowls, and the meat on a hot platter, with the accompaniments. *Serves 8 to 10, depending on the amount of meat*

Potée *(Peasant Pork and Cabbage Soup)*

The ingredients of this peasant soup vary from region to region, but cabbage and pork parts always appear. There are many pork products to choose from: garlic sausage (that fine Lyonnaise cervelas), shin of fresh pork, streaky salt pork, smoked pork, both fat and lean, ham, bacon, fresh pork butt or breast, and so forth.

1 cup dried white beans
4 cups water
3 pounds lean fresh pork
2 quarts boiling water
Freshly ground pepper

6 juniper berries, crushed
2 cloves garlic, crushed
2 tablespoons goose fat or butter
1 cup chopped onions
1 whole onion stuck with 4 cloves

1 carrot, sliced
1 leek, sliced
1 stalk celery, sliced
1 cervelas (garlic sausage)
Salt
1 cup sliced green beans
1 medium-sized cabbage, cut in
  eighths

8 potatoes, peeled

ACCOMPANIMENTS

Beer or red or white wine
Dijon mustard
Black bread and butter

Wash the beans and soak overnight in the 4 cups of water in a soup kettle. Three hours before dinner, boil the beans 1 hour; then add the fresh pork and the salt pork and 2 quarts of boiling water. Bring to a simmer and skim. Add the pepper, juniper berries, and garlic. Brown the chopped onions in the goose fat or butter and add to the soup with the whole onion and the sliced carrot, leek, and celery. Cover and simmer 1½ hours. Add the sausage and salt to taste and the green beans, and after 10 minutes add the cabbage and potatoes and cook 25 minutes more. Drain out the pork, sausage, cabbage, and potatoes and put them on a large hot platter. Serve the soup in bowls. *Serves 8*

Hotch Potch *(Scottish)*

2 to 3 pounds neck of lamb
2½ quarts boiling water
1 cup diced onions
1 cup diced carrots
1 cup peeled diced white turnips
2 leeks, sliced
Salt and pepper
1 cup fresh broad beans

2 cups fresh peas
1 cup green beans cut in ½-inch
  lengths
6 green onions, chopped
1 small cauliflower, separated into
  flowerets
2 cups shredded lettuce

Put the lamb in a soup kettle, cover with the boiling water, bring to a simmer, and skim. Add the onions, carrots, turnips, and leeks. Cover and simmer 1½ hours, then add the salt and pepper and the broad beans and cook another ½ hour. Add the peas, green beans, green onions, cauliflower flowerets, and the shredded lettuce, and cook 20 minutes more. Serve the meat on a hot platter along with bowls of soup containing vegetables. This is a fine soup when the vegetables are young and fresh. *Serves 6 to 8*

Hochepot *(French Hotch Potch)*

2 pig's feet
1 cup chopped onions
2 whole onions, each stuck with 2
    cloves
1 cup chopped carrots
2 cloves garlic, crushed
6 quarts water
2 or 3 pounds rump or chuck of beef
2 or 3 pounds breast of veal
Bacon fat
1 small celery root (celeriac), diced
2 white turnips, peeled and diced
2 leeks, sliced
½ small cabbage, shredded

Salt and pepper
1 potato per serving
1 garlic sausage
10 small pork sausages

GARNISH

Chopped chives or parsley

ACCOMPANIMENTS FOR MEATS

Mustard
Pickles
Alsatian wine or beer
Black bread and butter

You'll need a large kettle for this. Wash the pig's feet well and put them in the kettle with the onions, carrots, garlic, and water. Cover, bring to a boil, and skim, then simmer 1½ hours. Brown the beef and the veal in the bacon fat. Add the beef to the kettle, simmer ½ hour, then add the veal and cook 1½ hours. Then add all the vegetables except the potatoes and the garlic sausage, and after 10 minutes add the small sausages, cook 20 minutes. (A timer is especially useful for this recipe.) Remove the potatoes and all the meats and heap them on hot platters. Put the soup in small bowls, garnished with chives or parsley, and serve the meats, potatoes, and accompaniments at the same time. *Serves 8 to 12, depending on the amount of meat*

La Soupe Tourangelle *(Turkey Soup)*
Charles Barrier, Restaurant Le Negre, Tours, France

If you are visiting the château country, you will make a big mistake if you skip Tours. It is a charming city and this three star restaurant is one of the pleasantest places to dine in France. M. Barrier grows his own vegetables and serves fish and game from the region.

Turkey (back, wing and leg bones)
    with meat
½ cup shredded carrots
½ cup chopped onions
½ cup chopped celery
½ cup butter

3 tablespoons flour
1 cup dry white wine (Vouvray)
2 quarts hot water
Salt and pepper
Lump of butter

GARNISH

**Slices of turkey liver sautéed in
  butter
Wing meat of turkey**

ACCOMPANIMENT

Buttered croutons or toast

In Europe turkey is not necessarily roasted; the raw meat is often cut into slices and cooked; so this turkey soup is unlike ours. Brown the turkey parts and the vegetables in the ½ cup butter, then stir in the flour. Add the wine, hot water, some salt and pepper, and cover, and simmer gently 1½ hours. Strain the soup, add the lump of butter, and correct the seasoning. Dice the wing meat and add to the soup, with the sautéed slices of liver. Serve with buttered croutons or buttered toast. *Serves 6 to 8*

Wooden-Leg Soup (*La Soupe à la Jambe de Boua*)
Auberge Paul Bocuse, Lyon

M. Bocuse says: "This old recipe from the traditional gastronomy of Lyon is an illustration of a healthy cuisine where the savor and proper aroma of each ingredient is kept without pretension and in the peasant manner. Even the old spelling of *bois*—boua—is kept in the title. Serve Beaujolais without restraint. *Bon appetit."*

BROTH

**Shin of beef
4 quarts hot water
2 onions, sliced
1 whole onion stuck with 4 cloves
2 carrots, chopped
Bouquet garni: thyme, chervil,
  parsley, bay leaves
½ teaspoon each clove, cinnamon,
  ginger, and nutmeg**

VEGETABLES AND MEAT

**Salt and freshly ground pepper
2 leeks, minced
2 parsnips, sliced
2 white turnips, peeled and sliced**

**2 stalks celery, sliced
1 small leg of lamb
3 veal knuckles with meat
1 fresh pork butt
1 thick slice tender beef
1 partridge
1 young 3-pound chicken
2 turkey wings or legs
1 pair calf's brains, stuck with
  pistachios and truffle sticks and
  wrapped in cheesecloth
Garlic sausage (optional)**

ACCOMPANIMENT

**Red wine
Black bread and butter**

One might say that this soup is a French version of an Italian *bollito*. Some of the meats can be omitted but the one indispensable ingredient is the shin of beef which stands erect in the pot (whence the name) when two strong men bring it to the table.

Put all the broth ingredients in a very large soup kettle and simmer, covered, 45 minutes, until you have a good broth. Add the salt and pepper, the vegetables, lamb, veal knuckles, and pork butt. Cover, bring to a simmer, and skim well. Cover and cook gently 1 hour, then add the tender beef, the birds, and the turkey parts. Simmer gently another hour, adding more boiling water if necessary. Meanwhile soak the brains in salt water 1 hour, remove the membranes, and stick the nuts and truffles into the brains. Wrap in cheesecloth and tie securely. Lay the package on top of the soup and cook 20 minutes. Check the seasoning. A garlic sausage may be added at the same time as the brains. Have plenty of red wine and black bread and butter on hand. Drain out the meat, put it on hot platters, and carve. Serve the soup in bowls at the same time. *A great dish for practically any number*

Poule-au-Pot *(Chicken in the Pot)*

BROTH

2 veal knuckles, cracked, with meat
Chicken soup parts (wings, backs, necks, giblets)
2-½ to 3 quarts cold water
2 carrots, sliced
1 large onion, thinly sliced
4 whole cloves
1 leek, sliced
1 white turnip, peeled and sliced
½ teaspoon cinnamon
Salt and freshly ground pepper
Bouquet garni: thyme, parsley, 2 or 3 bay leaves

FARCE

¼ cup currants
½ cup Madeira
½ cup chopped onions
⅓ cup butter
½ pound chicken livers, sliced
Salt and pepper
1½ cups cubed rye bread, toasted
1 teaspoon anise powder

THE FINISHED SOUP

1 5-pound young corn-fed chicken
1 cup dry white wine
½ cup vermicelli

Make the broth first. Put the veal knuckles and chicken parts in the cold water, bring to a simmer, and skim. Add the rest of the broth ingredients, cover, and simmer 2 hours. Meanwhile, soak the currants in the Madeira 1 hour. To make the farce, sauté the onions in the butter until they begin to soften, then add the sliced livers and cook 2 minutes. Season with salt and pepper. Toss the cubed, toasted bread in the mixture, sprinkle with anise, and add the wine and currants. Stuff the chicken and tie it securely. Add the white wine to the broth and put in the chicken on its side. Cover and cook 30 minutes at the gentlest simmer. Turn the chicken onto the other side and continue cooking 15 minutes, then turn it on its back for another 15 minutes. For a plump young bird, an hour is enough. Remove the chicken and wrap it in wax paper to keep it moist and warm. Strain the soup and cook the vermicelli in it 15 minutes. Serve the soup in cups and the chicken separately. *Serves 6 to 8*

Turkey Wing Soup

6 or 8 medium-sized turkey wings
1½ cups sliced celery and leaves
1 cup sliced carrots
1 cup sliced onions
2 parsnips, sliced
1 white turnip, peeled and sliced
1 teaspoon basil
1 teaspoon thyme

1 teaspoon chervil or tarragon
1 can vegetable juice
1 cup dry white wine
Water to cover
Salt and pepper
2 tablespoons cornstarch
1 cup cream
½ cup Madeira or port

Now that some shops sell turkey parts this makes a fine dish for 6 or 8. Put all the ingredients up to and including the water in a large soup kettle. Cover, bring to a simmer, and cook gently 1 hour, then add the salt and pepper. Continue cooking until the wings are tender. If the vegetables are diced very fine you may not want to strain the soup. Blend the cornstarch with the cream, add a little of the soup, then combine with the rest of the soup and cook until it thickens a little. Serve the wings on plates accompanying the bowls of soup. *Serves 6 to 8*

Hungarian Lamb Soup

2½ pounds neck or breast of lamb
3 tablespoons mixed bacon fat and butter
1½ cups chopped onions
1 tablespoon flour
2 tablespoons sweet Hungarian paprika
2 teaspoons cumin powder

4 cups boiling water
½ teaspoon thyme
Salt and pepper
½ pound green beans
½ pound potatoes
1½ cups salted water
1 cup sour cream
1 cup egg noodles (optional)

Cut the lamb in 1½-inch cubes. Melt the bacon fat and butter in a heavy pot and cook the onions until they soften, then stir in the flour and paprika. Stir the cubes of lamb in this 3 or 4 minutes. Add the cumin and the boiling water. Cover and simmer gently 1¼ hours. Add the thyme, salt, and pepper. Meanwhile wash the beans and cut in ½-inch lengths. Peel the potatoes and cut in ½-inch cubes. Cook them together in salted water and when tender add them and their cooking water to the meat.

The meat should now be tender. Stir in the sour cream and reheat. Do not cook long after adding the cream. If the noodles are used, cook them separately in boiling salted water and add to extend this nourishing dish. Serve in wide soup plates. *Serves 6*

Boiled Beef with Buckwheat Grits *(Kasha)*

3 pounds rump of beef	1 teaspoon savory
2½ to 3 quarts boiling water	1 teaspoon marjoram
1 cup diced onions	1 cup buckwheat grits
1 whole onion stuck with 3 cloves	Salt and pepper
1 white turnip, peeled and diced	
1 parsnip, diced	ACCOMPANIMENTS
1 tablespoon tomato paste	Dijon mustard
1 leek sliced	Cucumber and lettuce salad
2 bay leaves	

Put the meat in a large soup kettle and pour 2½ quarts of boiling water over it. Bring it to the simmer and skim well. Add all the other ingredients except the grits, salt, and pepper. Cover and simmer gently 2 hours. Boil up the grits in 2 cups of water and add to the soup with salt and pepper. Cover and cook very slowly 1 more hour. Serve the soup and beef as separate courses. If the soup is too thick, add a little boiling water. This is a very nourishing winter dish. *Serves 6 to 8*

Boiled Beef and Vegetables with Soup or Aspic

This dish has always been considered in Europe one of the great ways of serving beef.

3 quarts rich beef stock	6 whole small parsnips
2 pounds bones	6 medium-sized potatoes
1 veal knuckle, split	Salt and pepper
4 pounds round or rump of beef	
Juice of 1 lemon	ACCOMPANIMENTS
1 onion stuck with 3 cloves	Sardellan sauce, Dijon mustard, and
6 whole white onions	cream horseradish
6 whole young carrots	Black bread and butter
6 whole white turnips, peeled	

Bring the stock, bones, and knuckle to the boil, then add the whole piece of beef and skim carefully. Add the lemon juice and the onion stuck with cloves. Cover and simmer gently 1¾ hours. Prime beef should be tender after the whole vegetables have been cooked with it for another

½ hour. In a separate pot bring the onions and carrots to a boil, drain and add them to the stock. After 15 minutes boil up the rest of the vegetables, drain, and add. In another 15 minutes they should be done. If necessary add salt and pepper to the broth. Remove the meat and vegetables and put them on a large hot platter and serve with a choice of sauces. Serve the soup in small bowls at the same time. Black bread and butter and a good Beaujolais will be welcome.

Brisket makes a wonderful boiled beef. Since it is quite fat, when it is to be served with aspic, the broth must be sieved, chilled, and the fat completely removed, then refrigerated until firm. Slice the meat and surround with chopped aspic. *Serves 6, hot or cold*

Bolliti Bolognese *(Boiled Meat and Vegetables)*

CHOICE OF MEATS (FOUR OR MORE)

1 fresh beef tongue or 3 veal tongues	1 teaspoon basil
3 pounds rump or round of beef	1 teaspoon thyme
1 calf's head with gristle	Salt and pepper
2 or 3 pounds fillet of veal	
2 pounds fresh pork butt	GREEN SAUCE
1 3-pound young chicken	1 cup parsley and watercress,
1 zampone or Czech sausage	ground
2 cups chopped onions	2 tablespoons sugar
2 cups chopped carrots	¼ cup lemon juice
2 white turnips, peeled and diced	2 tablespoons vinegar
1 whole onion stuck with 3 cloves	⅓ cup olive oil
1 large can vegetable juice	2 cloves garlic, crushed
2 cups dry white wine	12 capers
Boiling water to cover	⅔ cup meat broth
2 tablespoons chopped parsley	Salt and pepper

If the list of meats seems formidable, this is a restaurant choice. In Italy a steam table is brought around, with the meats in broth and a cutting board on which your choices are carved. One of the delicacies is the gristle from the calf's head. The housewife will choose the meats she fancies; there should be at least four kinds. This is a great dish for a big party.

If beef tongue is used put it in the kettle first, as it takes 4 hours to be really tender. Add the vegetables, vegetable juice, wine and boiling water to cover. Add the other meats according to cooking time: allow 3 hours for the beef, and 2 hours for the calf's head, veal tongues, fillet of veal, and pork butt. Add the herbs and salt and pepper 1 hour before the dish is done. The sausage takes 30 minutes. Boil the chicken separately 45 to 50 minutes. Serve the meats on platters. Strain the soup and serve in bowls. Mix the Green Sauce ingredients and serve in a tureen. As accompaniments serve beer and red wine, black bread and butter. *The full amount will serve 25 to 30*

Brazilian Peasant Soup

3 pounds neck or breast of lamb or
   rump of beef
3 quarts boiling water
1 3½-pound young chicken
1½ cups fresh corn
2 green peppers, seeded and sliced
1 pound potatoes, cubed
1 cup cubed pumpkin or squash
1 zucchini, sliced

1 tomato, skinned and sliced
2 onions, sliced
2 cloves garlic, crushed
1 cup sliced green beans
¼ cup minced parsley
⅓ cup Patna rice
Dash cayenne pepper
Salt and pepper

Put the lamb or beef in a large kettle and add the boiling water. Bring to a boil and skim. Cover and cook gently 2 hours, then add the chicken and all the other ingredients. Simmer gently 45 minutes to 1 hour, or until the chicken is done. Remove the meat and chicken to a hot platter. Serve the soup in bowls. *Serves 8 to 10*

Cabbage Soup with Spareribs

Spareribs for 4
Caramel
Salt and pepper
1 cup chopped onions
8 whole white onions
2 carrots, cubed

8 small new potatoes
1 new cabbage, quartered
2 teaspoons caraway seeds

ACCOMPANIMENT

Dijon mustard

Cut the spareribs in 4-inch squares or have the butcher do it. Paint them on both sides with caramel and sprinkle with salt and pepper. Lay ribs in a dripping pan and braise them for 20 minutes at 375°. Put them on the bottom of a soup kettle and add the chopped onions, whole onions, and carrots. Scrape out the dripping pan with boiling water and add the liquid to the soup kettle, then add boiling water to just cover. (Two teaspoons of chicken soup concentrate may be added to improve the flavor.) Cover and simmer gently 20 minutes. In a separate pot, bring the potatoes and cabbage to a boil, drain, and add to the top of the soup so that they will steam tender. Sprinkle with the caraway seeds. Cover and cook for 20 minutes. Drain the vegetables and spareribs and arrange them on a large hot platter. Season the soup with salt and pepper and serve it in bowls. *Serves 4*

Cock-a-leekie

I am sure the present-day Scot prefers a young tender chicken to a cock.

1 large bunch leeks	8 cups chicken stock
3 tablespoons butter	1/3 cup barley
1 young 3½-pound chicken	12 to 15 large sweet prunes
Salt and pepper	

Trim the leeks of tough outer leaves and use as much of the green as possible. Cut them in ½-inch lengths. Sauté ¾ cup of leeks in the butter until tender, then scrape them into the soup kettle. Add the chicken, the rest of the leeks, a little salt and pepper, the stock, and the barley. Cover and simmer gently 45 minutes. Add the prunes and cook 10 minutes longer. Remove the chicken, carve it, put the meat in a warmed tureen, and pour the hot soup and prunes over it. Serve in wide soup plates. Hot cornbread and butter are good with this. *Serves 6*

Congee *(The Porridge-Soup of China)*

This Chinese pot-au-feu is a kettle of fragrant, nourishing rice, millet, or barley with all sorts of meats and poultry added—a dish children and adults may dip into for morning breakfast to midnight snack. The kettle sits on the back of the stove where it may be replenished from time to time. Carcass of roasted chicken, turkey, or duck; spareribs or other pork meats; fresh meat and leftover meat—anything too good to discard is used. Here is a version for an American housewife with many mouths to feed.

Choice of veal knuckle with meat, neck of lamb, spareribs, breast of veal	10 to 12 cups of water
	Fresh herbs, minced, or dried herbs
	1 tablespoon salt
Chicken soup parts (wings, backs, necks, giblets)	Chopped onions, carrots, and other vegetables
1½ cups, or more, millet, brown rice, buckwheat grits, pearl barley, or steel-cut oats	GARNISH
	Finely sliced green onions

Put all the ingredients in a large soup kettle and let simmer 2½ hours. Chicken soup concentrate may be added for more flavor. Stir from time to time and keep the heat as low as possible. Experiment to find out which grain is the most popular with your family. Steel-cut oats are marvelous, especially if they are browned a little first in a dry heavy pot. You may want to add whole vegetables to the top 30 minutes before meal time. Porridge-soup is delicious with finely sliced green onions sprinkled over each serving. *Serves any desired number*

Cream of Veal Soup

4 pounds breast of veal
1 cup diced onions
1 cup diced carrots
1 white turnip, peeled and diced
1 parsnip, scrubbed and diced
1 cup sliced celery
1 large leek, sliced
1 teaspoon thyme
2 teaspoons tarragon
1 cup dry white wine
8 cups water

3 teaspoons chicken soup concentrate
½ cup fine breadcrumbs
1 tablespoon mixed dried herbs
½ pound button mushrooms
3 tablespoons butter
2 tablespoons minced onion
1 cup heavy cream
½ cup grated Parmesan or Gruyère cheese
Salt and pepper

Here is a grand meal in itself. The veal is not boned; most of the bones drop out when it is cooked. Put the veal in a large kettle and add all the other ingredients up to and including the soup concentrate. Cover and simmer gently 2 hours or until the meat is tender. Remove the meat and bone it if necessary. Mix the breadcrumbs with the dried herbs and pat over the meat; put it in a pan and glaze it under the broiler. Strain the soup. Bake the mushrooms with the butter and onion 10 minutes and scrape into the soup. Boil the cream with the cheese and when the cheese is melted add the mixture to the soup. Check the seasoning. Serve the soup and meat separately. Chutney and mashed potatoes are good accompaniments for the meat. *Serves 6 to 8*

Near East Fête Day Soup *(Chicken Soup with Lamb Quenelles)*

2 2½-pound chickens
2 quarts water or more
2 tablespoons chicken soup concentrate (optional)
½ cup Patna or Indian rice
Pinch saffron or 1 teaspoon turmeric
Grated rind of 1 orange
2 tablespoons orange flower water
Salt and pepper
½ teaspoon cinnamon
3 tablespoons minced parsley

LAMB QUENELLES

4 ounces raw ground lamb
2 egg yolks
2 tablespoons grated onion
Salt and pepper
1 teaspoon oregano
2 tablespoons cornstarch

ACCOMPANIMENTS

Fruit chutney
Cooked vegetable

Put the chickens in a large kettle and add the water. The addition of 2 tablespoons chicken soup concentrate is suggested to give more flavor. Bring slowly to a simmer. Wash the rice and add it with all the seasonings except the cinnamon and parsley. Cook slowly for 45 minutes. Remove the chickens and add the cinnamon and parsley to the broth. Mix the ingredients for the quenelles and form into marble-sized balls. Add them to the broth, cover, and simmer gently 18 minutes. Serve the soup and chickens separately. *Serves 8 to 10*

Ham and Vegetable Soup

½ small sugar-cured ham
1½ cups chopped onions
1 cup chopped carrots
2 white turnips, peeled and diced
2 whole cloves
1 teaspoon marjoram
1½ quarts warm water

6 whole potatoes
12 large spinach leaves, minced
3 tablespoons butter
Salt and freshly ground pepper

ACCOMPANIMENT
Dijon mustard

Put the ham in a soup kettle and add the onions, carrots, turnips, cloves, and marjoram. Add 1½ quarts warm water, cover, and simmer gently 1½ hours. Boil up the potatoes, drain them, lay them on top of the soup, and continue cooking until they are tender, about 25 minutes. Drain out the potatoes and ham and keep them warm in a 250° oven. "Melt" the spinach leaves in the butter about 3 minutes. Purée the soup in a blender and add the spinach. Add salt and pepper if needed. Serve the soup separately and serve the mustard with the ham and potatoes. *Serves 6*

Mulligatawny

1 cup chopped onions
3 tablespoons butter
1½ tablespoons curry powder
½ cup chopped carrots
½ cup diced celery
2 sprigs parsley
2 pounds chicken legs and thighs,
  or 2 pounds neck of lamb, cubed
8 cups boiling chicken consommé
1 tart apple, cut in julienne sticks
1/3 cup Madeira or sherry
2 tablespoons cornstarch
Salt and pepper

ORIENTAL PILAF

1½ cups Patna rice or Indian rice
4 green onions, sliced thin
3 cups chicken broth
1/3 cup raisins or currants
¼ cup Madeira
1 teaspoon turmeric
1/3 cup flaked coconut
Lump of butter

ACCOMPANIMENT
Fruit chutney

Sauté the onions in the butter in the bottom of a soup kettle until they begin to soften, then stir in the curry powder. When mixed, stir in the carrots, celery, and parsley then turn the chicken or lamb in the mixture until it is well covered. Add the boiling consommé. (If water is used, mix in 2 tablespoons of chicken soup concentrate.) If chicken is used, cover and cook very gently for 30 minutes or until tender. Meanwhile soak the apple sticks in the wine. When the soup is done, remove the chicken and take all the meat from the bones. Blend the cornstarch with the apple-wine mixture and add it to the soup and when it thickens, return the chicken meat to the soup. Check the seasoning. If lamb is used, cook it 2 hours; do not remove from the soup. Add apple and cornstarch mixture as directed above. For the pilaf, soak the rice and onions in the 3 cups broth 1 hour before cooking. Soak the raisins or currants in the wine 1 hour. Cook the rice over very low heat, tightly covered, 10 minutes, then add the turmeric, coconut, fruit, and wine, and cook 10 minutes more. Add the butter. Serve the soup in wide soup plates, accompanied by the rice on small plates. Some of the rice may be spooned into the soup. *Serves 8*

Mutton Broth with Spinach *(Near East)*

2½ to 3 pounds neck of lamb	2 teaspoons crushed coriander
2½ quarts boiling water	berries
Soup concentrate (optional)	2 cloves garlic, crushed
½ cup Patna rice, washed	2 teaspoons cumin powder
1 cup finely chopped onions	Salt and pepper
4 tablespoons butter	1 pound fresh spinach

Cut the lamb in 1½-inch cubes and put it in a large soup kettle, add the boiling water, cover, bring to a simmer, and skim. Add 2 teaspoons of soup concentrate if you wish. Cook gently 1 hour. Add the rice. Sauté the onions in the butter and add them with the seasonings. Cover and cook 45 minutes. Meanwhile wash and trim the spinach and chop it very fine in a wooden bowl. Add to the soup and simmer another 30 minutes. Put some pieces of meat in each soup plate and ladle the soup on top. *Serves 6 to 8*

Philadelphia Pepper Pot with Dumplings

1 pound each of 3 kinds of tripe: black, honeycomb, and fat (gras double)
1 big onion, sliced
4 cloves garlic, sliced
1 veal knuckle with meat
2 onions, chopped fine
2 tablespoons each basil, marjoram, savory
3 quarts water
2 tablespoons flour
1 cup tomato purée
4 potatoes, diced
½ cup dry white wine
Salt and pepper

DUMPLINGS
¾ cup cornmeal
1 cup sifted white flour
2 teaspoons baking powder
1 teaspoon salt
2 tablespoons chopped chives or chopped green onions
2 tablespoons sour cream
1 egg, beaten
¼ cup buttermilk or more

Have the tripe cleaned and scraped by the butcher. The day before making the soup, wash the tripe and scald and rinse it three times with boiling water. Put it in the soup kettle, add the sliced onion and the garlic, cover with water, and simmer gently 6 hours, covered. Drain the tripe and cut it in ¾-inch squares. Three hours before dinner, put the tripe in a soup kettle with the veal knuckle, chopped onions, herbs, and 3 quarts water. Cover and simmer 2 hours. Remove the knuckle, cut the meat in small pieces and return the meat to the kettle. Brown the flour and blend it with a little of the broth, then add it to the soup with the rest of the ingredients. For the dumplings, sift the dry ingredients together and stir in the chives or onions. Mix the beaten egg, sour cream, and ¼ cup of buttermilk, and combine with the flour mixture, adding just enough buttermilk to make a soft but stiff dough. When the potatoes are almost done, drop the dumplings by tablespoonfuls into the soup. Cover tightly and simmer gently 12 to 15 minutes. Serve dumplings, one or two in each plate of soup. *Serves 8 or more*

Scotch Broth #1

⅔ cup dried split peas
2 cups water
3 pounds shoulder or neck of lamb
4 beef marrow bones
2½ quarts boiling water
1 cup barley
1 large onion, diced
1 cup diced carrots
½ cup sliced celery
Salt and pepper
2 bay leaves
1 teaspoon marjoram
1 small cabbage, shredded, or 2 cups shredded kale
2 carrots, cubed
2 tablespoons chopped parsley

Wash the peas and soak in 2 cups of water 6 hours. Put the lamb and bones in a soup kettle, add 2½ quarts of boiling water, bring to a simmer, and skim. Add the peas and their soaking water, the barley, diced onion, and carrots, and the celery. Cover and simmer 2 hours. Add salt and pepper, the herbs, the cabbage or kale, and the cubed carrots. Continue cooking 30 to 40 minutes. Add a little boiling water if necessary. Remove the meat and serve it on a hot platter. Add the chopped parsley to the soup and serve it in bowls. *Serves 8*

Scotch Broth #2

²/₃ cup dried split peas	3 tablespoons minced parsley
1½ cups water	
3½ pounds neck of lamb, or 1 small leg of lamb	CAPER SAUCE
3 quarts boiling water	1 tablespoon cornstarch
1 large onion, diced fine	1 cup light cream
Salt and pepper	Salt and pepper
1 cup finely diced carrot	Grated rind of 1 lemon
3 leeks, finely sliced	2 tablespoons lemon juice
1 bunch green onions, finely sliced	3 tablespoons capers
1 cup diced white turnip	2 tablespoons butter
1 cup finely diced celery hearts	1 egg yolk

Wash the peas and soak several hours in 1½ cups water. Put the meat in a soup kettle, add 3 quarts of boiling water, bring to a simmer, skim, and simmer 30 minutes, covered. Add the peas, barley, onion, salt and pepper. Cover and simmer 1 hour. Add all the rest of the broth ingredients except the parsley and simmer 1 hour longer. Since the soup is not strained, the vegetables must be finely diced. Put the meat on a hot platter. Add the parsley to the soup and serve in bowls. To make the caper sauce, blend the cornstarch with the cream until smooth and cook until the mixture thickens, then add the lemon rind, juice, and capers. When ready to serve, reheat the sauce, whisking in the butter and egg yolk. Serve in a sauceboat. *Serves 6 to 8*

Soupe à la Tête de Veau *(Calf's Head Soup)*

1 calf's head
Hot water to cover
1 large onion stuck with 3 cloves
1 onion, sliced
1 carrot, sliced
1 clove garlic, sliced
1 cup finely sliced celery
1 cup dry white wine

2 tablespoons wine vinegar
Salt and pepper
1 tablespoon chicken soup
  concentrate

ACCOMPANIMENTS

Gribiche or Vinaigrette sauce (see
  index)

Have the butcher thoroughly clean and split the calf's head. Soak it in cold water 24 hours, changing the water 3 times. When you are ready to cook it, blanch it in boiling water, drain, and rinse. Put the head in a soup kettle with all the other ingredients, adding hot water to cover well. Bring to a simmer and skim. Cover and cook gently about 1½ hours. As the water boils away, add more boiling water to keep the head just covered. When the meat is tender, remove it and take all the meat off the bones. Serve it with one of the sauces. The meat, gristle, tongue and brains are considered great delicacies. Some of the meat may be diced and added to the cups of soup, along with a slice of lemon dipped in ground parsley. Six cups of broth and 2 cups of diced meat make a fine aspic which can be chilled in a mold.

Calf's feet may be prepared the same way but take 3½ hours to cook. They also make a fine aspic. *Serves 6 or more*

Soupe Rouenaise *(Chicken Liver Soup)*

Carcass of a roast duck
4 cups beef or chicken broth
2 cups water
1 cup red wine
1 cup chopped onions
½ cup chopped carrots
Salt and pepper
2 white turnips, peeled and diced

1 teaspoon thyme
1 teaspoon basil
½ pound chicken livers
3 tablespoons butter or duck fat
3 tablespoons chopped parsley
1 jigger cognac or ½ cup Madeira
Diced duck meat (if available)

Pound and disjoint the carcass and put it in a soup kettle with any leftover dressing and gravy. Add all the ingredients up to and including the herbs. Cover and simmer gently 1½ hours. Sauté the livers lightly in the butter or fat, then slice them. Strain the soup, add the livers, and purée the mixture. Check the seasoning. Dice any duck meat that is available and add to the soup with the cognac or Madeira and the chopped parsley. *Serves 6*

Near Eastern Lamb or Mutton Soup

2 pounds neck or breast of lamb
¼ cup oil
2 tablespoons flour
Salt and pepper
2 teaspoons oregano
⅓ cup minced parsley
1 cup chopped onions
½ cup sliced celery

2 teaspoons cumin powder
½ teaspoon cinnamon
1 teaspoon fennel seeds or powder
2 cloves garlic, crushed
2 quarts boiling water
⅓ cup vermicelli
Juice of ½ lemon
2 egg yolks

Cut the meat into 1½-inch cubes, and shake them in a paper bag with the flour, salt, pepper, and oregano. Heat the oil in a soup kettle and brown the meat on all sides. Add all the ingredients up to and including the boiling water. Cover and simmer gently 1¾ hours. Add the vermicelli and cook 15 minutes longer. If the soup is too thick add a little boiling water. Beat the egg yolks with the lemon juice, put the mixture in the bottom of a warmed tureen and whisk the hot soup into it. Mutton can be used when it is available. Serve with a green vegetable or hot rice and chutney. *Serves 6*

Spanish Pot-au-Feu

1 cup chick peas
3 cups water, plus 2 quarts
1½ pounds neck or breast of lamb, cubed
1 thick slice of ham, cubed
1 cup diced onions
1 clove garlic, crushed
6 chicken legs with thighs

Salt and pepper
1 cup sliced green beans
2 teaspoons cumin powder
2 teaspoons oregano
2 tomatoes, skinned and sliced
6 Spanish sausages
Oil or butter

Wash the chick peas and soak overnight in a soup kettle in 3 cups of water. Add 2 quarts more water and the lamb to the kettle. Cover and simmer 1 hour, then add the ham and cook ½ hour longer. Add all the other ingredients except the sausages and fat. Cook 20 minutes. Brown the sausages in a little oil or butter, add them to the soup, and cook 20 minutes longer—this makes 2 hours and 10 minutes cooking time altogether. Serve the soup in bowls and serve the meats on a platter. *Serves 6*

Waterzoii *(Belgian Creamed Chicken Soup)*

This soup with a Persian name has long been a favorite in Belgium. Chef Pierre Rogalle of the Brussels Restaurant gave me this recipe some years ago.

2 2½-pound chickens
⅔ cup chopped onions
½ cup chopped carrots
Pepper
2 bay leaves
2 quarts hot chicken broth
Salt
⅓ cup butter

⅓ cup flour
1 cup heavy cream
½ cup carrots cut in julienne sticks
½ cup finely sliced leeks

ACCOMPANIMENT

Boiled Patna or Indian rice
Fruit chutney

Put the whole chickens in a soup kettle and add the chopped onions and carrots, pepper, bay leaves, and hot broth. Cover and simmer gently for 20 minutes, then add a little salt, and continue cooking about 30 minutes more. Meanwhile melt the butter in a pan and blend in the flour until smooth. M. Rogalle cooks the mixture in a very slow oven until it becomes ivory color, about 20 minutes—this is the secret of any fine-flavored sauce. When the chickens are tender, remove them and strain the soup. Scald the cream, blend a little of it in the flour mixture, stir until smooth, then add the rest of the cream. Add this to the soup. Cook the soup very slowly, uncovered, for 20 minutes, stirring occasionally. Have the heat so low that the soup barely bubbles. Steam the julienne carrots and the leeks in very little water until tender, then add them to the soup. Put the chickens back into the soup to reheat and bring the chickens and the soup to the table in a large tureen. The chickens are removed to a platter and carved and the soup is served in bowls. Pass hot rice and chutney. *Serves 8*

Hungarian Beef Soup

2 pounds round or rump of beef
⅓ cup butter and oil, mixed
1 cup chopped onions
2 tablespoons sweet Hungarian
   paprika
Salt and pepper
2½ tablespoons flour
1 cup red wine
3 cups water
1½ pounds potatoes, cut in ½-inch
   cubes

⅔ cup tomato purée
⅔ cup sour cream
Beef broth

GARNISH

Chopped parsley

ACCOMPANIMENT

Buttered noodles

Cut the meat in scant ¾-inch cubes. Heat the butter and oil with the onions in the bottom of a soup kettle until the onions soften. Stir in the flour. Mix the wine with the water, heat and add. Cover and simmer gently for 2 hours. Add the cubed potatoes and salt and pepper, and cook 30 minutes. Mix the tomato purée with the sour cream and add. Add enough broth to make a creamy soup consistency. Serve the soup in wide soup plates, sprinkling each serving with chopped parsley. Accompany with hot buttered egg noodles. *Serves 6*

A Viennese friend tells me that in the streets all over Vienna there were little covered pushcarts where the young revelers stopped for *Goulasch-Suppe* to steady their legs on their walk home since *die letzte Blaue* (the last street car, which shows a blue light) has long since gone. There was some unmelodic singing in the deserted streets around the *Goulasche-Hütte*. The young Sigmund Freud reported that he participated in this gustatory frolic on his way from the Institute.

French and Italian Provincial Soups

Soupe de Cahors (Goose-Neck and Onion Soup)

There are a number of these regional soups; the vegetables vary but goose fat is always used.

3 tablespoons goose fat
2 cups chopped onions
4 ounces sorrel, minced
4 cloves garlic, crushed
2 tablespoons flour

6 cups hot chicken consommé
2 tablespoons tomato paste
Neck or leg of preserved goose
  (confit d'oie) or fresh goose
3 egg yolks

Color the onions in the fat in a heavy pot and when they begin to soften, stir in the sorrel and garlic. Simmer gently a minute, then blend in the flour. Add the hot consommé, the tomato paste, and the goose. Cover and simmer gently 30 minutes. Beat the egg yolks in a warm tureen, pour in the hot soup, and beat with a whisk. Serves 6

Thourin (Vegetable Soup with Goose Fat)
Jean Moussie, Bistro 121, Paris

M. Moussie comes from Figeac in the Quercy; this is one of the soups of that region and a very fine one. The restaurant is one of the very popular ones in Paris. They have a dedicated clientele of Frenchmen as well as Americans. Some of the dishes are not to be found elsewhere; some are regional but all are of the highest quality and imagination.

4 medium-sized onions, chopped
4 cloves garlic, crushed
1½ pounds white turnips, peeled
  and sliced
1 pound snow peas (mange-tout)
1½ pounds tomatoes, skinned,
  seeded, and chopped
3 tablespoons goose fat or butter

2 tablespoons oil
2 quarts boiling chicken consommé
Salt and pepper
3 eggs, beaten

GARNISH

1 slice toast per serving

Stir all the vegetables in the goose fat and oil over low heat in a soup kettle until they are golden (M. Moussie says butter may be used but the goose fat gives the soup a fine and typical flavor. He adds that if water is used instead of consommé a little wine should be added). Add the boiling consommé to the vegetables, cover, and simmer gently 15 or 20 minutes. Check the seasoning. When ready to serve, reheat the soup. Stir a little of it into the beaten eggs and whisk the eggs into the soup. Use wide soup plates, put a piece of toasted bread in each, and pour the soup over it. Or, if you prefer, serve the toast separately. *M. Moussie says this serves 6; I say nearer 10*

Soupe Engadinoise *(Swiss Peasant Soup)*
Auberge du Lion d'Or, Cologny, Geneva

The soup was given me by M. Lacombe, chef-proprietor of this elegant restaurant. It is a soup of the mountain people. Serve it with dark bread and cheese—appenzeller would be a good one.

1 carrot, chopped	Pinch or two of salt
1 onion, chopped	1/3 cup pearl barley
2 leeks, thinly sliced	4 ounces dried beef, diced
1 white turnip, peeled and diced	
1/2 cup sliced celery	ACCOMPANIMENTS
3/4 cup butter	Dark bread
1/4 cup water	Cheese
6 cups boiling water	

Melt 1/3 cup of the butter in a soup kettle and stir the vegetables in it with 1/4 cup of water for a minute. Cover and let steam a little over low heat. Add the 6 cups of boiling water to the vegetables, with a little salt (the meat may be salty). Cover and cook over very low heat 40 minutes. Skim the soup. Add the barley and cook 30 minutes more. Meanwhile soften the meat in 3 tablespoons of the butter. Add it to the soup and cook 3 minutes. At the moment of serving, add the rest of the butter. *Serves 4*

Soup Provençale *(Provence Vegetable Soup)*

3 potatoes, peeled and diced	5 cups boiling chicken stock or water
3 large tomatoes, skinned and crushed	Salt and pepper
2 cloves garlic, crushed	1 small- to medium-sized eggplant
1/2 cup chopped onions	2 tablespoons butter
1/3 cup butter	2 tablespoons oil

Put the vegetables in a soup kettle with the ⅓ cup butter and stir for 3 minutes over low heat. Add the boiling stock or water (if water is used, add 3 teaspoons chicken soup concentrate). Cook covered, 15 minutes, then pureé the soup and add salt and pepper. Peel the eggplant, cut in ¾-inch cubes, and soak in salt water ½ hour. Rinse and drain on paper towels. Heat the butter and oil, toss the cubes in the fat until they color, and then bake them in a heavy pan 10 minutes in a 350° oven. Reheat the soup and add the eggplant cubes. *Serves 6 to 8*

Velouté Dominique *(Creamed Potato and Celery Soup)*
Maurice Cazalis, Henri IV, Chartres

I can't imagine going to France without visiting Chartres and I can't imagine going to Chartres without visiting the Henri IV, to see our friend Maurice Cazalis. Habits of twenty-five years are hard to break. These visits always pay with fresh and elegant culinary ideas.

4 large potatoes, peeled and diced
1 celery root, peeled and diced
1¼ cups water
Salt and freshly ground pepper
2 cups hot rich chicken stock
1 cup hot light cream

1 cup heavy cream
2 egg yolks

ACCOMPANIMENTS

Small croutons fried in butter
Bowl of grated Gruyère cheese

Put the potatoes and celery in a heavy pot with the water, salt and pepper and cook, covered, until vegetables are tender. Purée the contents of the pot and add the stock and light cream. Reheat to serve. Scald the heavy cream, mix with the egg yolks, and whisk into the pot. Do not let boil again. Serve with croutons and cheese. *Serves 6 to 8*

Soupe au Pistou *(Vegetable Soup with Pasta)*

This Provençal soup might be called the French version of minestrone. The usual method is to put many vegetables in a kettle of water, but I have found that cooking the vegetables separately and using chicken stock instead of water turns a good soup into a great one.

½ cup dried lima beans
1½ cups water
6 cups chicken stock
Butter
1½ pounds fresh peas
2 teaspoons basil
Salt and pepper
½ pound fresh green beans, cut into 1-inch lengths
½ teaspoon rosemary
1 or 2 small zucchini, sliced, but not peeled
1 small green pepper, cut in thin strips
6 white onions, sliced very thin
1 medium-sized tomato, skinned, seeded, and chopped, or ½ cup canned tomatoes

1 can white shoepeg corn, or 1 cup cooked fresh corn
1 clove garlic, crushed
½ cup small egg noodle shells

PISTOU SAUCE

6 large cloves garlic, crushed
Large handful parsley, chopped
½ cup olive oil
⅓ cup soup broth

GARNISH

Bowl of grated Parmesan cheese

Soak the lima beans in the water 4 or 5 hours, then cook them until they are tender and put them and their water in a large soup kettle and add the chicken stock. Cook the vegetables separately, adding them to the kettle with their cooking juices as they finish cooking. Put a pat of butter and ⅓ cup of water in a small heavy pot, add the peas, basil, salt, and pepper, cover tightly, and cook 8 to 10 minutes over low heat; a pressure cooker takes 1 minute. Cook the green beans, with a pat of butter, rosemary, salt and pepper, and water about 12 minutes in a heavy pot or 3 minutes in a pressure cooker. Put the zucchini in a heavy pot with the strips of green pepper on top, and steam 5 minutes covered. Sauté the onions in 3 tablespoons butter and 2 tablespoons water in a heavy covered pot. Add salt and pepper. If you can't get a home-grown tomato, use canned tomatoes and crush them. This is enough tomato as they are not to dominate the flavors. The corn is an American addition but a very good one. Add the garlic to the kettle. Cook the noodle shells in salted boiling water until tender, drain, and add them to the soup. For some unaccountable reason, when the soup is served a green pea will be nestling in each noodle shell.

For the pistou sauce put the crushed garlic in a mortar and stir the finely minced parsley into it with a pestle (pistou), then slowly add the olive oil and thin with broth. Season with a little salt and pepper. Reheat the soup and serve it in wide soup plates. Serve the pistou sauce out of the mortar at the table, putting a big tablespoon into each plate of hot soup. Its rising fragrance is tantalizing. Pass a bowl of Parmesan cheese to sprinkle over the top of each serving. *Makes 3 quarts and serves 10 to 12 (if 12 are to be served increase the quantity of ingredients for the sauce)*

Minestrone

This soup is as well known in this country as it is in Italy. It is always a great favorite with family and friends. It is thick with vegetables, greens, and pasta and is a meal in itself. Serve it with a green salad, cheese and fruit for dessert and plenty of good red wine.

1 cup chickpeas, kidney beans, or white beans
6 cups water
3 cloves garlic, crushed
Salt and pepper
3 strips bacon, cut in pieces
3 tablespoons butter or ham fat
1½ cups chopped onions
1 young carrot, thinly sliced
2 potatoes, diced
1 cup sliced celery
2½ quarts hot chicken stock
1 cup white wine
1 teaspoon basil
2 teaspoons marjoram
Grated rind of 1 lemon
Juice of ½ lemon

½ cup shredded fresh basil (if available)
2 cups tomatoes
2 cups shredded fresh spinach
1 small zucchini, sliced but not peeled
¾ cup tiny noodle shells or rotelle
2 tablespoons chopped parsley
½ cup Parmesan cheese, grated

GARNISH

3 or 4 sweet and 3 or 4 hot Italian sausages, cooked and sliced

ACCOMPANIMENT

Bowl of grated Parmesan cheese

Wash the chickpeas or beans and soak 6 hours or overnight in 6 cups of water. Boil them 1½ hours slowly, covered, with the garlic, adding some salt and pepper after 1 hour. Cut up the bacon and fry it in the butter or ham fat until it begins to brown. Stir the onions in the fat until they begin to soften, then add the carrot, potatoes, celery, and the hot stock, and the wine. Cover and cook gently 15 minutes. Add the beans and their cooking liquid. Add all the other ingredients except the parsley and cheese. Cover and simmer gently 20 minutes. Add a little more hot stock if needed. When the pasta is done, stir in the parsley and cheese. For the garnish, bake the sausages in a 375° oven, turning after 10 minutes, then baking 10 minutes more. If the oven is too hot, turn it to 325°. Cut the sausages in slices and add to the soup. Serve the soup in wide plates. Pass the cheese. *Serves 12*

Giuseppina's Minestra Matta *("MAD" Soup)*
Bologna

Giuseppina's family likes this soup which they call "mad" because it has no meat in it!

4 ounces streaky salt pork	**½ cup chopped onions**
2 tablespoons butter	**6 cups boiling chicken or meat**
¹/₃ cup minced parsley	**broth**
3 cloves garlic, crushed	

Slice the pork, then dice it fine. Put it in a heavy pot and sauté it in the butter until it is crisp. Stir in the parsley, garlic, and onions, cook for 3 minutes, then add the boiling broth. Simmer gently, covered, 20 minutes. Pass a bowl of grated cheese and one of croutons if you like. *Serves 6*

Fish and Seafood Soups

Fish Stock or Fumet #1

2 pounds fish trimmings: skin,
  bones, heads, shrimp shells (if
  available)
Salt and freshly ground pepper
Bouquet garni: 1 teaspoon thyme, 3
  sprigs parsley, 1 bay leaf
1 carrot, sliced

½ cup chopped onions
2 shallots, minced
2 whole cloves
2 stalks celery, sliced
1 cup dry white wine
1 pint clam juice
Water

If the fish man has shrimp shells, they give the stock a fine flavor. Put all the ingredients in a large kettle. If you are using the stock to poach fish in and to make a sauce to serve it with, skimp the water. If you are using the stock as called for in fish soup recipes, make the total liquid, including water, wine and clam juice, 2 cups more than the number of servings desired. For instance, if you are serving 6, use 8 cups of liquid to allow for evaporation in the cooking and sieving: 1 cup wine, 2 juice, and 5 water. Cover, and simmer at medium heat for 25 to 30 minutes. Strain the stock. It is then ready to use. *Makes 1½ quarts or more, depending on the water used*

Fish Stock or Fumet #2

3 tablespoons butter
2 tablespoons oil
1 large onion, sliced fine
1 clove garlic, crushed
1 teaspoon salt
Freshly ground pepper
Mushrooms stems, sliced (optional)
6 cups water
1 cup dry white wine

1 pint clam juice
1 teaspoon thyme
3 sprigs parsley
1 teaspoon marjoram
Dash cayenne
3 pounds fish trimmings: bones,
  heads, skin, shrimp shells (if
  available)

Put the butter and oil in a soup kettle and cook the onion in it until it begins to soften. Add all the other ingredients, cover, and cook at medium heat 35 to 40 minutes. Strain the stock. *Makes over 1½ quarts*

Aigo Bouido *(Garlic Fish Soup)*

2 cups cubed potatoes
3 cloves garlic, crushed
2 tomatoes, skinned, seeded, and
    chopped
Grated rind of 1 orange
Pinch saffron
½ cup finely sliced celery
⅔ cup diced onions
½ teaspoon thyme
1 teaspoon powdered fennel

2 tablespoons minced parsley
Salt and freshly ground pepper
¼ cup olive oil
2 quarts water
3 pounds fillets of 3 kinds of
    white-fleshed fish

ACCOMPANIMENTS

Rouille (see index)
Thin rounds of toast

Put all the ingredients except the fish in a fish cooker. Cover and cook gently 20 minutes. Put the fillets on the cooker rack, lower into the broth, and simmer 12 minutes or until fillets are done. Drain the fish onto a hot platter. The fish may be served separately along with soup in wide plates, or some of the fish may be added to the soup. Pass a bowl of *rouille* to spread on the toast to accompany the soup, or a toast round with *rouille* may be put into each soup plate. *Serves 6*

Anchovy Soup

2 large leeks, minced
1 cup diced onion
1 clove garlic, crushed
1 white turnip, peeled and diced
2 tablespoons butter
Oil from can of anchovies
Pinch of salt
Freshly ground pepper
½ cup tomato purée

2 or 3 cups chicken broth
1 pint clam juice
1 small can anchovies, drained and
    cut in ½-inch lengths
3 tablespoons chopped parsley

ACCOMPANIMENT

Bowl of small croutons fried in
    butter

Sauté the vegetables in the butter 2 or 3 minutes. Add the other ingredients except the anchovies and parsley. Cover and cook gently 18 minutes. Add the anchovies and parsley. Serve with a bowl of croutons. A cup of small diced potatoes may be cooked with the vegetables if desired. *Serves 4*

Bouillabaisse à la Marseillaise
Le Drouant, Paris

This old distinguished restaurant has always specialized in fish dishes, especially a bouillabaisse which is as authentic as you will find in Marseilles itself. Jules Petit, Chef de Cuisine, kindly gave me this recipe. The fish used there are French species; we may use fresh cod, sea bass, sole, red snapper, bluefish, eel, lobster, and shrimp.

FISH STOCK

Fish trimmings
Shrimp shells
1 onion, chopped
1 teaspoon each thyme, savory, and
    rosemary
Salt and pepper
2 quarts water
2 cups good dry white wine
1 stalk celery, sliced
1 leek, sliced
3 sprigs parsley

THE SOUP

½ cup olive oil
1 cup chopped onions
White part of 2 big leeks, sliced
Grated rind of 1 orange
2 big tomatoes, skinned, seeded,
    and crushed

2 cloves garlic, crushed
Big pinch saffron
1 branch fennel
1 bay leaf
Salt and pepper
5 pounds mixed fish fillets
1 pound shrimp
2 1½-pound lobsters, split and cut
    in pieces

ROUILLE

2 cloves garlic, crushed
2 red pimentos, mashed
Lobster coral
2 tablespoons fine breadcrumbs
1/3 cup olive oil
1/3 cup fish stock
Dried French bread or toast

The fish man will give you the heads, skin, and bones of the fish. Put them in the kettle with the shrimp shells and other stock ingredients, cover, cook 30 minutes, strain, and set aside. Half an hour before you intend to serve the soup, put ¼ cup of the olive oil in the kettle, add the soup vegetables, cover, and slowly soften them without letting them burn the least bit. Add all the other soup ingredients. Put the firmest fish on top of the vegetables and pour in the strained stock adding a little water if necessary to cover. Cover and simmer very gently. Put the pieces of lobster in a separate pan with the other ¼ cup of olive oil and cook until lobster is red, then add 1 cup stock or water and cook, covered, 15 minutes. When the firmest fish has simmered 15 minutes, add the more delicate-fleshed fish to the kettle, and simmer gently 8 minutes. Add the shrimp and cook 1½ minutes. Meanwhile, mix together the ingredients for the rouille, (which is necessary to make this a grand dish) until the texture is like mayonnaise. When the lobster is cooked, add it and its broth to the soup. Spoon the rouille into the soup or spread it on dried French bread or toast. Each soup plate should contain a piece of fish, a piece of lobster and 1 or 2 shrimp. If you have a handsome copper kettle, serve the soup from it at the table. *Serves 8 to 10*   ·

Bouillabaisse Froide en Gelée *(Cold Bouillabaisse in Aspic)*
Jacques Lacombe, Auberge au Lion d'Or, Cologny, Geneva

This is a jellied version of bouillabaisse for summer. For this M. Lacombe uses 1 pound each filleted St. Pierre, rascasse, sole, baudroie, grondin. American alternatives are listed in the ingredients. This superb French restaurant is a short drive from Geneva and overlooks the lake. It is in the tradition of the Troisgros brothers and Paul Bocuse.

1 pound each fillets of sole, pike, perch, bass, trout, brill, whitefish
Juice of 1 lemon
½ cup French olive oil
1 pound fresh shrimp

FISH STOCK

Fish trimmings
Shrimp shells
1 leek, sliced fine
½ cup fresh fennel, chopped fine
1 carrot, chopped
1 onion, chopped fine
3 cloves garlic, crushed
2 tomatoes, chopped
6 cups water

VEGETABLES

¼ cup olive oil
½ cup water

1 small carrot, cut in julienne sticks
1 small leek, sliced fine
½ cup fennel, cut in julienne sticks
4 tomatoes, skinned, seeded, and chopped
1 teaspoon saffron
3 teaspoons orange rind, cut in julienne sticks
Salt, pepper, cayenne
3 sprigs parsley, chopped
Fresh chervil, chopped

ACCOMPANIMENTS

Rouille
Mayonnaise made with lemon juice
Small rounds of toast

Marinate the fish fillets 1 hour in the lemon juice and ½ cup olive oil. Shell the shrimp and reserve. To make the stock, put the fish trimmings and the shrimp shells in a kettle with all the other stock ingredients and 6 cups water. If you wish, add enough good dry white wine to cover. Cover and cook 25 minutes. Strain through a fine sieve. The fish bones provide the aspic. To cook the garnish vegetables, put the ¼ cup of the olive oil and ½ cup water in a heavy pot, add the carrot, leek, and fennel, cover, and cook until the vegetables begin to soften. They must be crisp and fresh. Skin, seed, and crush the 4 tomatoes, and put them in a fish cooker. Add the fish fillets, sprinkle with the saffron, and add the julienne vegetables, orange sticks, salt, pepper, and a dash of cayenne. Moisten with a little fish stock and simmer 7 or 8 minutes, adding the shrimp for the last 1½ minutes. Cool a little. Oil individual terrines. Arrange in each a piece of fish, a shrimp, some of the vegetables and orange sticks, and tiny sprigs of parsley and chervil. Fill the terrines with broth and chill until firm. For *rouille* see index; there are several recipes in the book. Pass the *rouille,* a bowl of mayonnaise, and small rounds of toast. *Serves 8*

Burgundy Fish Stew

FISH STOCK

Fish trimmings: bones, heads, skin
1 quart water
1 lemon, sliced
Pinch sage
2 cloves garlic, crushed
1 carrot, sliced
1 onion, sliced
3 whole cloves
1 teaspoon thyme
1 teaspoon sugar
2 bay leaves
Salt and pepper

THE STEW

¼ pound salt pork, diced
2 cups sliced onions

3 cups cubed potatoes
2 cups canned tomatoes
4 pounds filleted freshwater fish:
    pike, pickerel, bass, trout, or other
Dash cayenne
2 cups Burgundy
Salt and freshly ground pepper

GARNISH

8 slices French bread sautéed in
    olive oil with crushed garlic

If possible, use 4 kinds of fish. Put all the stock ingredients in a kettle, cover, cook 25 minutes, then strain. Fry out the diced salt pork in a fry pan and scoop the pieces into the bottom of the soup kettle. Add the onions to the pork fat and after a minute add the potatoes and cook until they are well colored. Put alternate layers of fish and of the cooked vegetables and the tomatoes in the soup kettle. Check the seasoning of the stock and add the cayenne. Heat stock with the Burgundy and pour into the soup kettle. Cover and cook very gently 30 minutes. If carefully cooked the fish will keep its shape. Slice the bread a good inch thick. Heat the olive oil in a skillet with the crushed garlic and fry the slices of bread in the oil. Put a slice in each wide soup plate and ladle the fish and broth over it. *Serves 8*

Red Snapper and/or Sea Bass Chowder

FISH STOCK

Trimmings from filleted fish
1 cup water
1 pint clam juice
1 cup dry white wine or dry
** vermouth**
1 onion, thinly sliced
1 carrot, thinly sliced
1 stalk celery, sliced
1 teaspoon thyme
1 leek, sliced
1 clove garlic, crushed
Salt and pepper

THE CHOWDER

2 slices salt pork, diced
2½ pounds fish fillets
2 cups diced onions
2 cups cubed potatoes
Salt and freshly ground pepper
½ cup fresh cracker crumbs
1 cup heavy cream
2 egg yolks

Make the stock with all the ingredients. Cover and cook 25 minutes, then strain and set aside. If you cook the chowder in a porcelain-lined casserole, the casserole may be brought to the table. Put the salt pork in the bottom of the cooker and fry it out a little. On the pork put alternate layers of fish, onions, and potatoes, and cracker crumbs. Lightly season each layer of fish and vegetables. Pour in the strained stock, cover, and cook very slowly 40 minutes. If this is cooked gently the fish won't break too much. Scald the cream, mix with the egg yolks, and pour over the top of the chowder. Lift the pieces of fish into hot soup plates and add the soup. This is one of the most delicious fish soups. *Serves 4 to 6*

Hungarian Fish Soup

⅓ cup oil and butter, mixed
1 cup chopped onions
2 tablespoons sweet Hungarian
** paprika**

Salt and pepper
2 pounds fish fillets
6 cups boiling fish stock
½ cup sour cream

Put the oil and butter in a fish cooker and cook the onions in it until they soften. Stir in the paprika and add salt and pepper. Remove half of the onions and reserve. Lower the fish into the kettle on the rack, cover with the reserved onions, and add the boiling stock. Cover and simmer gently 20 minutes. Drain out the fish and put it into a warmed tureen. Purée the contents of the soup kettle, reheat, stir in the sour cream, and pour the hot soup over the fish. Any freshwater or saltwater fish may be used. *Serves 6*

Indochinese Fish Soup

FISH STOCK

Fish trimmings and shrimp shells
2 quarts water
Salt and pepper
1 onion, sliced
1 tablespoon minced fresh ginger
   root

THE SOUP

Pinch saffron or 1 teaspoon turmeric

¼ cup vermicelli
2 pounds fresh fillets of fish:
   whitefish, sole, bass, perch
½ cup sliced green onions
12 or 18 fresh shrimp, shelled

GARNISH

12 fresh pineapple sticks
3 tablespoons mixed butter and oil

Make the fish stock with all the stock ingredients including the ginger root and cook it 25 minutes, covered. Strain the stock; you should have 6 cups. Put the strained stock in a fish cooker and add the saffron or turmeric and the vermicelli. Bring to a boil, then lower the fish on the rack into the stock and scatter the green onions over the fish. Cover and simmer gently 10 minutes, then add the shrimp and cook 2 minutes more. Meanwhile prepare the pineapple (only fresh will do, as the canned is too sweet). Cut into sticks and sauté in the butter and oil until they are golden on all sides. When the fish is done, drain it out and divide it into warmed wide soup plates. Put 2 or 3 shrimp and 2 sticks of pineapple in each plate. Ladle the soup over the fish. *Serves 6*

Matelote à la Bourguignonne *(Burgundian Fish Soup)*

SAUCE

1 bottle red Burgundy
⅓ cup finely diced onion
¼ cup grated carrots
2 tablespoons minced shallots
2 whole cloves
½ teaspoon thyme
Bouquet garni: parsley, bay leaf,
   chervil
1 tablespoon brown sugar
¼ cup breadcrumbs
2 cloves garlic, crushed
½ teaspoon meat extract
Salt and pepper

THE FISH

3 pounds fish fillets: trout, pike,
   perch
1 jigger cognac
4 ounces fresh mushrooms
2 tablespoons lemon juice
3 tablespoons butter
Beurre manié: 2 tablespoons each
   butter and flour, mixed

GARNISH

6 canapés of French bread fried in
   butter
Chopped parsley

Put all the ingredients for the sauce in a fish cooker, cover, and cook it 30 minutes, then strain through a sieve and put it back in the cooker. Put the fish on the rack and blaze it with cognac, then lower it into the sauce. Cover and cook gently until the fish begins to flake, about 12 to 15 minutes. Meanwhile clean the mushrooms, sprinkle them with lemon juice, and sauté 5 minutes in the butter. Remove the fish and keep it warm. Put bits of the beurre manié in the simmering sauce to thicken it. Fry the bread until golden. Put a piece of bread in each hot soup plate, top with a piece of fish, and divide the sauce over it. Sprinkle with chopped parsley. Two pounds of fresh sliced salmon may be cooked the same way. A white Burgundy may be used in the sauce. Serve the same kind of wine you used in the sauce. *Serves 6*

Oriental Fish Soup

PILAF

1½ cups Indian or Patna rice
3 cups chicken stock
⅓ cup sliced green onions
1 clove garlic, crushed
½ teaspoon each cinnamon and mace
1 teaspoon cardamom, coriander, turmeric, and cumin powder, mixed
Salt and pepper
Big lump of butter

4 rings fresh pineapple, cut in segments (do not use canned pineapple)
2 tablespoons fresh onion juice
1 large ripe tomato, skinned, seeded, and crushed, or ⅓ cup tomato purée
1 teaspoon basil
1 teaspoon coriander
Dash cayenne
2 pounds firm fish fillets

THE SOUP

6 cups chicken stock
Salt and pepper

Begin the pilaf first. Put all the ingredients except the butter in a heavy pot. Cover tightly and bring to the boil, then turn the heat to pilot-light strength and simmer the pilaf 25 minutes. Stir in the butter. For the soup, put all the soup ingredients except the fish in a fish cooker and cook 5 minutes, then lower the fish on the rack into the soup, cover, and cook slowly 15 minutes. Carefully lift the fish into a hot tureen and pour the soup over it. Put a large spoonful of pilaf in each warmed soup plate and ladle the fish fillet and soup over each. Serve the rest of the pilaf in a bowl. *Serves 6*

Portuguese Fish Soup

FISH STOCK

Shrimp shells
Fish trimmings
Grated rind of 1 lemon
Juice of 2 lemons
½ cup chopped onions
1 clove garlic, crushed
2 bay leaves
1 teaspoon coriander
Salt and pepper
1 carrot, sliced
6 cups water

THE SOUP

¼ cup olive oil
½ cup tomato purée
1 quart mussels
1 pound shrimp
1¼ cups white port wine
2 pounds fish fillets: eel, ray, and
   whitefish

ACCOMPANIMENTS

Rouille (see index)
Small rounds of toast

Shell the shrimp, set them aside, and put the shells and all the other stock ingredients into a large kettle. Cover, cook 30 minutes, and strain. Add the olive oil and tomato purée to the strained stock. Soak the mussels 1 hour in cold water, then scrub them with a rough brush to remove all moss and grit. Put the mussels in a kettle with the wine and steam them, covered, 2 or 3 minutes until they open, then shell them over the wine to save the juices. Put the mussels aside. Strain the wine and juices to remove any grit and add them to the stock. Put the stock in the soup kettle. Put the fish on a rack, lower into the stock, and cook about 10 minutes, add the shrimp and cook 1½ minutes longer. Drain out the fish and shrimp, add the mussels, and put all into a hot tureen and pour the boiling stock over them. Pass *rouille* to spread on toast and to spoon into the soup. *Serves 6*

Red Snapper Soup with Sorrel or Watercress

FISH STOCK

Fish trimmings
½ cup chopped onions
½ cup chopped celery
½ cup chopped carrots
1 leek, finely sliced
1 pint clam juice
Salt and pepper
1 teaspoon thyme
Juice of ½ lemon
1 cup dry white wine
4 cups water

THE SOUP

1 cup sorrel or watercress
2½ pounds red snapper fillets
¼ cup butter
¼ cup fine fresh breadcrumbs
2 egg yolks

ACCOMPANIMENT

Bowl of croutons fried in butter

Put all the stock ingredients in a pot, cover, and simmer 25 minutes. Strain it. Chop the herb quite fine in a wooden bowl. Soften it in the butter, then add to the strained stock and the bread crumbs. Put the stock in a fish cooker, lower the fish into it on a rack and cook about 12 minutes or until fish is done. Drain out the fish and serve it on a hot platter. Blend a little stock with the yolks, then whisk into the stock. Serve the soup in cups at the same time. Scalloped potatoes are a good accompaniment for the fish. Pass the croutons. *Serves 6*

Thomas Tew's Newport Fish Chowder

This old recipe had long been a secret until a Newport friend gave it to me some years ago. Sea bass or even pike or trout may be used if blackfish is not available.

3 to 4 pounds blackfish (tautog)
2 quarts water
4 ounces salt pork, diced
4 cups diced onions
1 quart can tomatoes
4 cups diced potatoes
¼ teaspoon sage
1 teaspoon thyme
1 teaspoon basil
½ teaspoon cloves
2 dashes cayenne pepper

¼ teaspoon black pepper
1 teaspoon sugar
Salt to taste
1 lemon
Clam juice or water
1 cup claret or Burgundy
1 tablespoon butter

ACCOMPANIMENT

Pilot crackers

Have the fish cleaned and scaled but left whole with the head on. Put the fish in 2 quarts of water and simmer gently until it is tender (about 35 minutes), then remove it. Save the water. Remove the meat from the bones and set it aside. Discard skin, head, and bones. Fry the salt pork in the bottom of the fish kettle until golden, add the onions, and cook until onions begin to soften, then add the tomatoes, potatoes, all the seasonings, and the fish water. Cut a thin slice from each end of the lemon and then slice it thin. Cook it 15 minutes in ½ cup of water, covered, then add the lemon slices and their water to the soup. Put the fish back into the soup and add as much clam juice or water as needed to serve 8. Set the kettle on low heat to ripen several hours before serving. Reheat the soup and add the wine and butter; do not let boil again. Serve with pilot crackers. *Serves 8*

Turtle Consommé with Madeira

This is an elegant party soup.

1 quart can turtle consommé	ACCOMPANIMENT
1 can turtle meat	Cheese straws (see index)
¹/₃ to ½ cup Madeira	

GARNISH

Chopped parsley

Heat the consommé and turtle meat in a saucepan. Add the wine and ladle into hot cups. Garnish with chopped parsley. The consommé and meat may also be added to clear rich beef stock to serve a large number of people. Cheese straws are the usual accompaniment. *Serves 6*

Soupe au Poisson à la Rouille *(Fish Soup with Rouille)*
Capucin Gourmand, Nancy

Georges Romain, the director-chef of this great restaurant, gave me the recipe for this rich soup, which is quite unlike the soups of the Mediterranean.

4 pounds fish: (pike, trout, perch, bass, sole), cut in pieces	1 quart mussels, cleaned and shelled
1 tablespoon tomato paste	2 ounces pasta shells, cooked
Salt	
Green part of 2 leeks, sliced	ROUILLE
1 clove garlic, crushed	3 cloves garlic, crushed to a paste
1 onion, minced	2 egg yolks
1 teaspoon basil	1¼ cups olive oil
2½ quarts water	2 canned red pimentos, mashed
¾ cup olive oil	¼ cup fish broth
White part of 2 leeks, sliced	Dash cayenne
1 onion, minced	
5 cloves garlic, crushed	ACCOMPANIMENT
1 pinch saffron	
¾ pound tomatoes, skinned, seeded, and crushed	Grilled croutons

Have the fish cleaned, scaled, and cut in pieces. Put it in a soup kettle with the next seven ingredients. Cover and cook gently 1 hour to obtain a good fish fumet. In another pot put the olive oil, white part of the leeks, and the onion and cook until the vegetables soften without coloring. When the fumet has cooked 1 hour strain it into the vegetables through a sieve. Remove and discard all skin and bones and press as much of the fish as possible through the sieve. Add the garlic, saffron, and tomatoes and cook another hour. At the last moment add the mussels and cooked noodle shells. The *rouille* is made like mayonnaise: whisk the eggs, garlic, and oil together, adding the oil drop by drop. Add the mashed pimento and fish broth. Put a big spoonful of *rouille* in each soup plate. Pass the croutons. *Serves 8*

Soupe de Poissons du Maître *(Fish Soup with Fennel)*
Chope d'Orsay, Paris

This recipe is a specialty of Chef Jacques Fils. Jean and Andrée Boutersuy, hosts of this very special small restaurant, are a welcoming pair and have a most devoted clientele.

3 pounds fish: perch, sole, halibut, eel, bass, fresh cod
1 cup chopped onions
2 carrots, diced
1 bulb fennel, sliced
1 cup chopped celery
2 cloves garlic, crushed
2 leeks, sliced
1/3 cup olive oil
Big pinch saffron
1 cup tomato purée
Dash cayenne

Salt and pepper
2 teaspoons thyme
3 bay leaves
1 cup white wine
2 tablespoons tomato paste
2 quarts water or more

ACCOMPANIMENTS

Rouille (see index)
Bowl of grated Gruyère cheese
Toast

Have the fish cleaned. It is not filleted but cooked with the bones and heads. Cut the small fish in 2½-inch pieces and the big fish in slices. Stir all the vegetables in the olive oil in a large kettle over low heat for 3 minutes, then stir in the fish. Add the rest of the ingredients, cover, and simmer as gently as possible for 2 hours. Add a little boiling water if necessary. Discard the fish heads, skin, and bones and press as much of the fish through a sieve as possible. Check the seasoning and add more cayenne if you like. The *rouille* and cheese are passed in bowls along with the toast. *Serves 8*

Cod Stew

3 tablespoons butter
2 slices salt pork, diced
1 cup diced onions
1½ cups diced potatoes
2 pounds fresh cod fillets
Salt and pepper
5 cups milk

3 teaspoons chicken soup
    concentrate
2 egg yolks

ACCOMPANIMENT

Croutons fried in butter

Put the butter and pork dice in the bottom of the soup kettle and fry the pork until crisp. Stir in the onions and potatoes and cook 3 minutes. Lay the fish on the vegetables and add a little salt and pepper. Boil up the milk with the soup concentrate and pour it over the fish. Cover and simmer gently 20 minutes. Purée 2 cups of the liquid and vegetables in a blender and add to the egg yolks. Put a piece of fish in each heated soup plate. Add the purée to the soup, reheat, and divide the soup over the fish. Serve a bowl of croutons fried in butter. *Serves 6*

Anguilles au Vert *(Eel Soup with Herbs)*
Grand Hotel, Brussels

M. Gablin, director of the hotel, gave me this Belgian specialty. Its goodness partly depends on the fresh herbs. These must be hand-chopped in a wooden bowl. Three or four of them will be enough.

3 pounds eel, cleaned and skinned
⅓ cup butter
¼ cup minced shallots
½ cup minced onions
1 glass dry white wine
6 cups hot chicken consommé or
    fish stock
1½ cups chopped fresh herbs:
    sorrel, chervil, burnet, sage,
    parsley, watercress, tarragon

2 tablespoons cornstarch
1 cup heavy cream
6 egg yolks, beaten
Salt and pepper
Juice of 1 lemon

ACCOMPANIMENT

Crisp buttered toast

Cut the eel in 3-inch lengths. Cook it gently in the butter with the shallots and onions for 5 minutes, stirring the pieces of eel until they color golden on all sides. Add the wine, consommé or stock, and the herbs. Cover and cook gently 15 minutes. Do not overcook, for the eel must not fall apart. Blend the cornstarch with a little of the soup, then add it to the rest of the soup. Reheat the soup. Scald the cream and stir it into the beaten egg yolks. Dip some of the soup into the cream mixture, then whisk the mixture into the soup. Heat without boiling and add the seasoning and lemon juice. Serve in heated wide soup plates, putting a piece of eel in each. Pass crisp buttered toast. A fine white Burgundy is the best wine to serve with this elegant soup. *Serves 8*

Matelote d'Anguilles au Vin d'Arbois
(Eel Soup with Rosé Wine)
Chez Maître Paul, Paris

This small restaurant has been one of our favorites in Paris. Its devoted clientèle comes here for the famous ris de veau (sweetbreads), chicken dishes, and, in fact, everything they serve, not to mention the welcome of friendly M. et Mme. Gaugain.

2¾ **pounds eel**
Oil and butter
2 **carrots, sliced in thin rounds**
2 **onions, sliced in thin rounds**
1 **jigger cognac**
3 **cloves garlic, crushed**
1 **bottle (3½ cups) Arbois rosé wine**
1 **cup fish stock**
Beurre manié: 2 tablespoons flour
   mixed with 2 tablespoons soft
   butter

GARNISHES
Croutons fried in butter with
   crushed garlic
12 **small white onions, cooked**
Bacon crumbles

Have the eel cleaned and skinned, and cut it in 2½-inch lengths. Wash it in cold water and wipe it dry with paper towels. Stir it quickly in oil and butter until it is golden on all sides, being careful not to burn it. Put a big lump of butter in the casserole in which you plan to serve the dish and add the onions and carrots. Add the pieces of eel and blaze with cognac. Add the garlic. Stir the mixture over low heat for a few seconds, then add the wine. (M. Gaugain comes from Jura, as do the lovely wines he cooks with. A rosé from the Loire may be substituted.) Cook 15 minutes, then remove the eel to a platter and cover it loosely with wax paper. Put the sauce in the top of a double boiler over simmering water and cook it, uncovered, 1 hour. Add the fish stock. Sieve the sauce and thicken it with little pieces of beurre manié. Cook the sauce 5 minutes. Add the eel to the sauce, heat, then lift the eel pieces into the casserole, and pour the sauce over it. Garnish the dish with croutons, white onions, and crisp bacon crumbles. *Serves 6*

Anguilla alla Moda *(Eel Soup à la Mode)*
Attilio Volcan, chef, Piromallo, Bologna

3 pounds eel, skinned, boned, and
   filleted
Flour, salt, and pepper
4 tablespoons vegetable oil
1 jigger cognac
½ cup dry white wine
2 medium-sized onions, finely diced
4 tablespoons butter
6 ounces mushrooms, chopped

1 clove garlic, crushed
2 tablespoons chopped parsley
3 tablespoons olive oil
2 tomatoes, skinned and chopped
6 cups hot chicken consommé
½ cup thick cream

GARNISH

Slices of toast

Roll the eel lightly in seasoned flour and cook in the vegetable oil until golden. Put it in a 350° oven for 6 minutes, then add the cognac and wine. Meanwhile sauté the onions in the butter over low heat for 5 minutes. Cook the mushrooms, garlic, and parsley in the olive oil in a soup kettle 2 minutes, stir in the tomatoes, and add the onions. Put the eel and its juices on the vegetables and add the hot consommé. Handle the eel carefully so as not to break it. Simmer gently 15 minutes. Stir in the thick cream. (The cream used in Italy is as thick as *crème fraiche.*) Put a piece of toast in the bottom of each warmed wide soup plate, top with a piece of eel, and ladle the soup over it. *Serves 6 to 8*

La Bourride *(Marseilles Fish Soup)*
Vieux-Port New York, Marseilles

We went to Marseilles in quest of yet another "authentic" bouillabaisse but were very lucky that our hosts, Francois and Pierre Venturini, persuaded us to take their specialty, this *bourride*. Its delicacy and flavor are not to be described. It is worth a trip to Marseilles, and when you get there hurry to the Vieux-Port New York.

COURT BOUILLON

1 onion, sliced
1 carrot, sliced
1 fennel bulb, sliced
2 bay leaves
1 tablespoon minced parsley
Salt and peppercorns
6 cups water

AIOLLI SAUCE

6 cloves garlic
4 egg yolks
3 tablespoons wine vinegar
Salt and pepper
2½ cups peanut oil
2 tablespoons boiling water

FISH TO SERVE 4

Sea bass or sea perch
4 slices halibut

Whiting
1 baby lobster, quartered
¼ cup olive oil

THE SOUP

½ cup heavy cream, reduced to ¼ cup
2 egg yolks
Half the aiolli sauce
½ clove garlic, crushed
The strained court bouillon

ACCOMPANIMENT

Rounds of toast fried in garlic butter

Put the ingredients for the *court bouillon* in a kettle, cover, cook 25 minutes, and strain through a sieve. Meanwhile make the aiolli sauce. Have the ingredients at room temperature. Crush the garlic to a paste, add the egg yolks, and blend until smooth. Add the vinegar, salt, and pepper. Add the oil, drop by drop, whisking continuously, until the sauce begins to thicken, then by teaspoons until the mixture is thick enough to add it a little faster. When it becomes a thick mayonnaise, add the boiling water to make it smooth. Have the fish cleaned and left whole. Lower it on a rack into the court bouillon, cover, and cook it gently 15 minutes. The original recipe calls for *langouste*, but since that is not found in American waters, baby lobster is substituted. Stir the lobster quarters in a sauté pan with the olive oil until they turn red, then cover and cook slowly for about 15 minutes or until the meat is tender. Drain the fish from the *court bouillon* and put it and the lobster on a hot platter and keep warm. Reserve the *court bouillon*. Boil ½ cup heavy cream 15 minutes to reduce to ¼ cup. Put the cream in a pot with the egg yolks, half the aiolli sauce, and the crushed ½ clove garlic and whisk until blended, then whisk into the hot *court bouillon*. Put the soup through a sieve. Reheat without boiling and serve in hot soup plates, along with the fish, which is served on side plates. Serve the rest of the aiolli sauce in a bowl to spread on the toast, or add some of it to the soup. This is a complete meal. *Serves 4*

Bourride or Bouillabaisse Blanche *(White Bouillabaisse)*
Petit Navire, Paris

This soup from Provençe calls for rockfish; the nearest American equivalents are red or black rockfish, striped bass, log perch, and some of the groupers—whitefish living on the rocky bottoms. Marcel Gilot, now retired, gave me this fine recipe some years ago. People came from all over Paris for this soup.

FISH STOCK

5 pounds assorted fish
Fish trimmings
1 large onion, chopped
1 tomato, skinned and seeded
½ cup olive oil
2 tablespoons minced parsley
2 bay leaves
2 teaspoons savory
1 teaspoon oregano
2 cloves garlic, crushed
2 teaspoons powdered fennel
Salt and pepper
2½ quarts boiling water
Big pinch saffron

ROUILLE

**1 tomato, skinned and crushed, or 1
    tablespoon tomato paste**
5 cloves garlic, crushed
2 red pimentos, mashed
3 tablespoons olive oil
½ cup fish broth
Dash cayenne

GARNISH

French bread rubbed with garlic

Have the fish man skin and fillet the fish and give you all the trimmings: heads, skin, and bones. Put the trimmings with all the stock ingredients except the saffron in a soup kettle, cover, and cook for 25 minutes. This may be made in advance and let stand to ripen. When ready to make the soup, strain the stock, reheat it, add the saffron, and lower the fish on a rack into the stock. Cover and cook for 10 minutes. Mix the *rouille*. Put a piece of garlicked bread in the bottom of each hot soup plate, top with a piece of fish, ladle in the soup. Add a spoonful of *rouille* to each plate and serve the rest in a bowl. *Serves 10*

New Orleans Shrimp and Crab Gumbo

THE FISH

2 pounds shrimp
1 pound cooked fresh crabmeat
1 pint oysters

FISH STOCK

Shrimp shells
1½ pounds fish trimmings
2 bay leaves
2 whole cloves
1 onion, sliced
1 carrot, sliced
1 teaspoon thyme
Salt and pepper
2 quarts water
1 pint clam juice

THE GUMBO

1½ pounds fresh okra
¼ cup butter

¼ cup bacon fat
2 cups finely chopped onions
½ cup thinly sliced celery
2 tablespoons tomato paste
2 cloves garlic, crushed
1 green pepper, sliced
½ cup flour
1 cup tomato purée
½ teaspoon Tabasco sauce
1 teaspoon Worcestershire sauce
1 quart chicken stock
1 tablespoon gumbo filé
3 tablespoons chopped parsley

ACCOMPANIMENT

Rice pilaf (see index)

Shell the shrimp and put them aside. Put the shrimp shells and the other stock ingredients in a kettle, cover and cook 1 hour, then strain. Cut off the tips of the okra, discard tips, and freshen the okra by rinsing in hot water with a pinch of soda, then rinse well in clear water, and dry. Melt the butter and bacon fat in a saucepan, add the okra, and toss until it begins to color. Remove the okra and reserve. Add all the other vegetables and stir them in the fat until the onions begin to soften. Add the flour, stir until it is smooth, then add the tomato purée. Stir in a little of the fish stock and add the sauces. Scrape the vegetable mixture into the fish stock and add the okra and the chicken stock. Bring to a simmer, cover, and cook gently 1 hour. Just before it is done, add the shrimp, cook a minute, and then add the crab meat and oysters. When the soup is very hot stir in the gumbo filé. This is dried sassafras, a thickening agent, and the soup must not boil after it is added. Add the parsley to the top. Serve immediately, accompanied by rice pilaf. *Serves 10*

Shrimp Bisque #1

FISH STOCK

Shrimp shells
Salt and pepper
1 teaspoon thyme
1 cup dry white wine
½ cup chopped onions
¼ cup diced carrots
2 whole cloves
1 teaspoon marjoram
4 cups water
2 teaspoons chicken soup
   concentrate
1 pint clam juice

THE BISQUE

2 pounds fresh shrimp
3 tablespoons butter
Salt and pepper
1 jigger brandy
½ cup tomato purée
1 cup heavy cream
2 egg yolks

Wash the shrimp and shell them. Cut up the shells with kitchen scissors and put them in a kettle with the other stock ingredients. Cover and simmer 25 minutes, then strain through sieve. Cook the shrimp in the butter a minute until they turn pink, season, and blaze with brandy. Reserve one shrimp for each serving; cut these in half lengthwise and put 2 halves in each soup plate. Add the tomato purée. Purée the rest of the shrimp in a blender with 2 cups of stock, rinse the blender with another cup of stock, and add both to the rest of the stock. When ready to serve, reheat. Scald the cream, mix it with the egg yolks, and whisk into the soup. Do not let boil after the cream is added.

To extend this soup, put a 1-pound slice of salmon in 2 tablespoons butter and 1 cup of water or half water and half wine, cover and cook very gently 6 to 8 minutes on each side. Skin and bone the salmon and purée it with its liquid, adding some broth if necessary. This is combined with the puréed shrimp. If the soup is too thick add clam juice and a little wine. *Serves 8 to 10*

Shrimp Bisque #2 (With Quenelles)

QUENELLES

1 cup heavy cream
1 pound raw shrimp, puréed
Salt and pepper
2 egg whites

THE SOUP

1½ pounds fresh peas
½ cup water
1 teaspoon basil
1 cup carrot juice
1 cup vegetable juice
2 teaspoons cornstarch

1 cup cream
1 pound fresh shrimp
1½ cups water
Salt and pepper
¼ cup finely chopped onions
½ teaspoon thyme
1 teaspoon marjoram
1 teaspoon chervil

GARNISH

Dark rum

Quenelles make a fine garnish for any fish soup. Start them the day before the soup is to be served. Boil the heavy cream 18 minutes uncovered, over a brisk flame, watching constantly so that it doesn't boil over. Refrigerate overnight. The next day, beat the thick cream into the purée and refrigerate 2 or 3 hours longer. When ready to cook the quenelles, mold them into ovals with 2 teaspoons, and cook them 2 minutes in the simmering soup (or cook them in boiling chicken stock), covered.

This bisque is very good with or without the quenelles. To make the soup, cook the peas in the ½ cup of water, with basil, salt and pepper. (The pressure cooker takes 1 minute.) Mash them with their liquid through a sieve or purée in the blender. Combine with the juices. Blend the cornstarch with the cream until smooth, cook until thickened, and add to the soup. Wash the shrimp and put them in a pot with the 1½ cups water, the seasonings, onions, and herbs. Cover and cook 1½ minutes. Remove the shrimp, and shell them. Reserve the shrimp. Cut up the shells and return them to the pot, adding the shells from the shrimp used in the quenelles. Cover, and cook 10 minutes. Sieve this broth into the soup, pressing it against the sides of the sieve. Cut the shrimp in half lengthwise. In each soup plate put several shrimp halves, 1½ tablespoons of rum, and 3 to 5 quenelles. Divide the soup over the shrimp. Any leftover shrimp may be chopped and added to the soup. If the quenelles are cooked in chicken stock and 2 cups of it are added to the soup, it will serve 8. Serves 6 to 8

Preparing Clams for Soup

Have the fish man scrub the clams and shuck them, or do it yourself. All the juice must be saved and strained through a sieve lined with a damp cloth. Separate the hard part of the clams from the soft and grind the hard part. Squeeze the black substance from the soft part and discard it.

Puréed Clam Soup

24 clams
8 cups fish stock, strained
1 cup heavy cream

3 egg yolks
Big pat of butter
Paprika

Open the clams and prepare as previously directed. Add the ground hard part of the clams to the fish stock. Remove the black substance from the soft part and purée the soft part with some of the stock and the clam liquor. Add the rest of the stock to the purée and heat before serving. Scald the cream, pour it over the egg yolks, and whisk into the soup. Do not boil again. Add the butter. Sprinkle paprika over the top of each plate of soup. *Serves 8*

Quick Clam Chowder

1/3 cup green onions, minced
3 tablespoons butter
2 cans condensed New England
    clam chowder
1½ cups milk
1½ tablespoons cornstarch
1 cup light cream
1 cup clam juice

1 can minced clams
1 can whole clams
1 teaspoon turmeric
1 teaspoon thyme
Freshly ground pepper
¼ teaspoon nutmeg
Scant teaspoon salt
1 pound fresh shrimp (optional)

Sauté the onions in the butter a minute and scrape them into a large mixing bowl (not metal). Empty the chowder into the bowl, rinse the cans with the milk, and add. (I prefer Snow's to any other brand.) Blend the cornstarch with the light cream and cook until it begins to thicken, then add it to the bowl. Add the clam juice. Sieve the juice from the 2 cans of clams into the bowl. Reserve the minced and whole clams (they toughen when cooked). Add all the seasonings. If shrimp are used, steam them in very little water 1½ minutes, shell them, and put them with the reserved clams. The chowder may stand in the bowl all day to "ripen." Reheat before serving and add the reserved clams and the shrimp if used. This is a grand soup. *Serves 10 or more*

New England Clam Chowder

25 round hard-shell clams
2 ounces salt pork, diced
1½ cups diced onions
4 good-sized potatoes, diced
½ teaspoon salt
1 pint clam juice
Freshly ground pepper

1 cup milk
1 cup heavy cream
Paprika

ACCOMPANIMENT

Pilot crackers

Prepare the clams according to previous instructions. Fry out the salt pork, scoop out the pieces, and reserve them. Fry the onions and potatoes in the pork fat until just tender and add the salt, clam juice, and pepper; cover and cook gently 10 minutes. Cut up the clams with scissors, add them to the pot, and simmer, covered, 15 minutes. Boil up the milk and cream and add. Add the reserved pork pieces. Serve in warmed soup plates and add paprika to the top of each soup plate. Serve with crackers. *Serves 4 to 6*

New York Clam Chowder

1 quart clams
4 ounces salt pork, diced
1 cup chopped onions
2 cups diced potatoes
½ cup ground celery
1 cup skinned, seeded, diced
    tomatoes

4 cups clam juice
2 tablespoons butter

ACCOMPANIMENT

Pilot crackers

Prepare the clams according to the previous instructions. Fry out the salt pork in the bottom of a soup kettle until crisp, scoop out the pieces and reserve them. Sauté the onions, potatoes, and celery in the pork fat about 5 minutes, stirring often; do not let them brown. Heat the clam juice, add the tomatoes and the ground part of the clams; cook gently 15 minutes. Add the soft part of the clams, cover, and cook slowly 4 or 5 minutes. Let stand several hours to ripen. Add the pork pieces and reheat. Serve in soup plates and pass the crackers. *Serves 6*

Rhode Island Clam Chowder

4 ounces salt pork, diced
2 large onions, diced
3 large potatoes, cubed
1 quart clams, shucked
1 pint clam juice
1 cup skinned mashed tomatoes or
    tomato purée
1½ cups light cream

½ cup heavy cream
2 egg yolks
2 tablespoons butter
Salt and pepper

ACCOMPANIMENT

Pilot crackers

Fry the salt pork in the bottom of the soup kettle until crisp. Drain out the pieces and reserve them. Put the onions and potatoes in the fat and cook until they are golden, being careful not to burn them. Heat the clam juice. Grind the hard part of the clams, add to the vegetables with the heated clam juice, and cook 15 minutes. Add the tomatoes and the soft part of the clams, cover, and cook slowly 10 minutes. Before serving, reheat the soup, scald the two creams, and mix with the egg yolks, whisk into the soup. Add the butter. Do not boil again. Add the pork pieces and check the seasoning. Pass the pilot crackers. *Serves 6 to 8*

Steaming Crabs for Soup or Other Dishes

Wash 12 crabs. Put 2 cups of water and 3 tablespoons of vinegar in the bottom of a soup kettle, bring to a boil, and put in the crabs. Cover and steam over low heat 25 minutes from the time they begin to boil. Pick the meat from the shells; the steaming facilitates this process. Female crabs in the laying season have eggs and fat in the points of the shells; these make the soup rich, but getting females is a matter of luck. Cooked crab meat is available in most fish markets but is more expense than raw crabs.

Crab Soup

1 pound cooked crab meat
1 white onion, diced fine
Grated rind of ½ lemon
1/3 teaspoon mace
4 tablespoons butter
2 cups boiling milk
Salt and freshly ground pepper

Dash cayenne
½ teaspoon Worcestershire sauce
2 cups heavy cream
3 egg yolks
2 tablespoons Madeira for each
    serving

Shred the crab meat quite fine and remove all bones. Put the onion, lemon rind, mace, and butter in the top of a double boiler and cook over simmering water 5 minutes. Stir in the crab meat and when it is hot add the boiling milk. Let it cook 10 minutes. Add the seasonings. Scald 1 cup of the cream, add, and let the soup stand several hours. When ready to serve, reheat, then scald the other cup of cream, add it to the egg yolks, then whisk into the soup. Put the Madeira in hot soup plates and add the soup.

VARIATION: Shrimp soup may be made the same way. Cook 1 pound shrimp 1½ minutes, shell and grind. Proceed as for Crab Soup. *Serves 6 to 8*

Cream of Scallops

FISH STOCK

2 **pounds fish trimmings**
Shrimp shells (optional)
1 **cup chopped onions**
3 **tablespoons butter**
1 **carrot, sliced**
1 **teaspoon each thyme, marjoram,**
    and turmeric
Salt and pepper
1 **cup dry white wine**
2 **cups clam juice**
5 **cups water**

THE SOUP

2 **tablespoons cornstarch**
1½ **pounds scallops**
3 **tablespoons butter**
2 **tablespoons lemon juice**
1 **cup heavy cream**
2 **egg yolks**
2 **tablespoons chopped parsley**

Ask the fish man for 2 pounds of fish trimmings—heads, bones, skin, and shrimp shells if he has them. Sauté the onions in 3 tablespoons butter in the bottom of a soup kettle until the onions soften, then add the fish trimmings and all the other stock ingredients. Cover and cook 30 minutes, then strain the stock. Blend a little of the stock with the cornstarch, then add it to the stock. Sauté the scallops in 3 tablespoons butter a minute, then sprinkle with the lemon juice. Bay scallops are the right size; large sea scallops will have to be cut in ½-inch cubes. When ready to serve the soup, reheat it. Add the scallops. Scald the cream, beat it into the egg yolks, and whisk into the soup. Do not boil again. Add the parsley. *Serves 8*

La Bisque de Homard *(Lobster Bisque)*
M. Paul Genin, Chez Pauline, Paris

M. Genin has many decorations including that of the *Academie Culinaire de France,* of which he is a member. The cooking here is a blend of Lyonnais and Burgundian, a rich and heady mixture. This popular restaurant is back of the Comédie Française.

2 1½-pound lobsters

MIREPOIX

6 tablespoons butter
½ cup diced carrots
1 cup diced onions
Salt and pepper

THE BISQUE

1/3 cup cognac
1 cup white wine

2 quarts fish stock, white stock or poultry stock
2 tablespoons tomato paste
5 fresh tomatoes, skinned and sliced (not hot-house tomatoes)
Bouquet garni: thyme, parsley, chervil
1/3 cup rice
¼ cup butter
1/3 cup heavy cream
Freshly ground pepper
¼ teaspoon cayenne

Have the lobsters cut in half. Remove the coral and liver, cream it, mash through a sieve, and set aside. Cut each lobster in 4 pieces. Put the mirepoix ingredients in a heavy pot and cook until hot, then add the lobster pieces. Stir until the lobster is bright red. Blaze with the cognac, then add the wine and reduce a little. Add the fish stock, white stock or poultry stock, tomato paste, tomatoes, and bouquet garni. Cover and cook gently 20 minutes. Remove the lobster pieces, pick out all the meat, cut it in good-sized slices, and set aside. Pound the shells as fine as possible and return them to the soup. Add the rice, cover, and cook very gently 30 minutes. Pass the soup through a coarse sieve, pressing against the sides to get as much as possible through. If any shells get through, it will have to be sieved again. Whisk in the creamed coral mixture, the ¼ cup butter, the cream, and the seasonings. Reheat and add the lobster slices. M. Genin suggests a dry champagne to accompany this. *Serves 6*

La Soupe aux Huitres *(Oyster Soup with Fried Oysters)*
Raymond Oliver, Le Grand Véfour, Paris

24 oysters	2 shallots, minced
¼ cup dry white wine	1 clove garlic, sliced
Flour	3 tablespoons butter
1 cup thick Soubise Sauce (see	Salt and pepper
index)	1 glass dry white wine
Anglaise: 1 egg beaten with 1	2 teaspoons minced fresh tarragon
tablespoon each water and oil (or	²/₃ cup *crème fraiche* (see index)
more), pinch salt	2 egg yolks
Fine fresh breadcrumbs	4 teaspoons brandy
1 8-inch crab	Oil for deep frying

Open the oysters and save all their liquor. Remove them from the shells and put them in a porcelain or glass casserole (never in metal). Add the oyster liquor and the ¼ cup wine. Heat without boiling, then let cool. Drain and dry the oysters on a clean cloth. Strain the cooking liquid through a sieve lined with a damp cloth to remove any grit. Measure the liquid and reserve it. String 6 oysters on each of 4 small wooden skewers. Dust ever so lightly with flour, then dip in Soubise Sauce, then in Anglaise, and finally in the crumbs. Reserve.

Wash the crab and remove the intestine under the eyes. Chop the crab 5 times across with a cleaver. In a casserole cook the shallots and garlic in the butter until they begin to color, then add the crab; stir with a wooden spoon until the crab browns. Season with salt and pepper. Add the reserved cooking liquid of the oysters, the glass of wine, and the tarragon. If the liquids do not make 4 cups, add fish stock or clam juice. Mix well, mashing the crab so it will release as much meat and juice as possible. Cover and simmer gently 20 minutes. Pass the mixture through a sieve, mashing and squeezing it against the sides. Return the soup to the casserole. Whisk the *crème fraiche* with the egg yolks and add the brandy. Deep-fry the skewered oysters in 375° oil until golden. Bring the soup to the boil and whisk in the cream mixture; reheat without boiling. Serve the soup in large warmed cups accompanied by the oysters on small hot plates. *Serves 4*

Raymond Oliver presides over this fine restaurant which the Wine and Food Society rates among the dozen best restaurants in the world. The Grand Véfour has one of the most beautiful settings anywhere, situated at the far end of the Palais Royal, coming from the Place Colette and the Comédie Française. The garden is rich in history; Louis XIV bathed in its fountain as a child. The Palais Royal has been the scene of all sorts of revolutionary events throughout the history of Paris, and history is still being made, as its buildings are now occupied by various government offices.

M. Oliver is a man of wide culture and scholarship. He is the author of many books and his personal library contains over 6,000 cookery volumes and manuscripts. His *La Cuisine* (Tudor Press) is a monumental work, one of the few written in French and translated into English that is simple and explicit enough for the American cook. Everyone interested in wine, food, and beauty should lunch or dine at Le Grand Véfour; it is part of the Paris experience.

Oyster Consommé

36 oysters
Oyster liquor, strained
Big lump of butter
6 cups well-seasoned chicken
  consommé
4 egg yolks, beaten

½ cup dry white wine (Pouilly or
  Sancerre), warmed

GARNISH

Chopped parsley

Have the fish man shell the oysters and save their liquor. Put the oysters and liquor and the butter in the top of a double boiler over hot water but with the heat turned off, so they will warm without cooking. When ready to serve, boil up the consommé. Beat the egg yolks, put them in a warmed tureen, and whisk in the wine, then add the boiling consommé. Add the oysters and their liquor. Sprinkle the top of the soup with parsley. Use good wine and drink the rest of the bottle while you eat the soup. *Serves 6 to 8*

Oyster Creole Gumbo

10 or 12 chicken parts: legs, thighs,
  breasts
1 ¾-inch-thick slice of ham, cubed
3 tablespoons butter
3 tablespoons flour
10 cups chicken stock
2 cups chopped onions
1 large green pepper, sliced
4 tablespoons butter
2 cloves garlic, crushed
1 cup sliced celery and leaves

1 small can tomatoes
1 teaspoon curry powder
Salt and freshly ground pepper
⅛ teaspoon cayenne
2 teaspoons thyme
2 teaspoons basil
1 pound fresh shrimp
1 pound fresh okra
24 oysters and liquor
1 tablespoon gumbo filé

Put the chicken and the cubed ham in a large soup kettle. Brown the 3 tablespoons butter and the flour in a saucepan, and when it is smooth add a little chicken stock. Pour the mixture over the chicken and ham, along with the rest of the stock. Sauté the onions and green pepper in the 4 tablespoons butter over low heat until they begin to soften, then add them to the kettle. Add the next 8 ingredients, cover, and simmer very gently 1 hour. Meanwhile wash the shrimp and boil them in salted water 1 minute. Drain and save the broth. Shell the shrimp, return the shells to the shrimp broth, cook 10 minutes, covered, then strain the broth into the soup kettle. Reserve the shrimp. Cut the tips from the okra, bring the okra to the boil with a pinch of soda, then rinse well. Put them in the soup 5 minutes before it is done. When the soup is done, remove the chicken, take all the meat from the bones, leaving it in large pieces, and return it to the soup. This may stand a couple of hours to ripen. When ready to serve, bring the soup to the boil, add the shrimp, the oysters and liqour, and the gumbo filé. (This is dried sassafras, a thickening agent.) Stir and serve immediately. Do not boil after the filé is added. This is a fine dish for a party. A pilaf may be served with it. *Serves 10 to 12*

Oyster Stew #1

FISH STOCK

½ pound fish trimmings
4 ounces fresh cod
1 cup chopped onions
1 cup chopped celery
½ cup shredded carrots
Salt and pepper
1 teaspoon thyme
½ teaspoon mace or nutmeg
1 cup dry white wine or dry vermouth
4 cups water or part water and part clam juice

THE STEW

Chicken broth
1 tablespoon cornstarch
1 cup heavy cream
30 oysters, shelled
Oyster liquor, strained
Paprika

ACCOMPANIMENT

Pilot crackers

Put the trimmings, cod, and the other ingredients up to and including the water or water and clam juice in a soup kettle. Cover, simmer gently 30 minutes, and strain through a sieve. Measure the stock and add enough chicken broth to make 6 cups. This rich broth makes a fine stew. Blend the cornstarch with the cream, cook until it thickens, and add it to the stock. When ready to serve, reheat the soup and heat the oysters with their liquor in the top of a double boiler over simmering water without cooking them. Put 5 oysters in each hot soup plate and pour the hot soup over them. Sprinkle with paprika and serve with Pilot crackers. *Serves 6*

Oyster Stew #2

6 cups fish stock made with 1 pint
   of clam juice and 2 cups of water
24 or 36 oysters
Oyster liquor, strained
1 cup good dry white wine
Salt and pepper
Dash cayenne
2 tablespoons butter

1 cup heavy cream
3 egg yolks

GARNISH

Chopped parsley

ACCOMPANIMENT

Pilot crackers

Make the fish stock and strain it. Put the oysters and their liquor in the top of a double boiler with the wine, seasonings, and butter. When you are ready to serve them up, heat the oyster mixture over simmering water and boil up the stock. Scald the cream, beat it into the egg yolks, then whisk the mixture into the hot stock. The oysters may be put into a hot tureen with the boiling soup poured over them or they may be divided among hot soup plates and the soup added. Sprinkle each serving with parsley. Serve with crackers. *Serves 6*

Southern Oyster Soup with Okra

½ cup diced onions
¼ cup bacon fat
2 ripe tomatoes, skinned and sliced
6 cups hot chicken stock
½ pound small fresh okra
2 tablespoons cornstarch

24 oysters
Oyster liquor, strained

GARNISH

Chopped parsley

Cook the onions in the bacon fat in the bottom of a soup kettle, until they color. Add the tomatoes and cook 2 minutes, then add the hot stock, cover and cook 15 minutes. Cut off the tips of the okra, bring the okra to the boil with a pinch of soda to brighten it, rinse well, add to the soup, and cook 5 minutes. Mix the cornstarch with a little of the soup until smooth, then add to the soup and bring it to the boil. Heat the oysters in their liquor in the top of a double boiler, then divide the oysters among warmed soup plates. Add the oyster liquor to the soup, then pour the soup over the oysters. Sprinkle parsley over each serving. *Serves 6*

Shellfish Stew

24 clams
1 pound shrimp

FISH STOCK

Shrimp shells
Fish trimmings
1 onion, sliced
1 carrot, sliced
2 cloves garlic, crushed
1 teaspoon savory
1 teaspoon thyme
1 teaspoon basil
Salt and pepper
1 pint clam juice
1 cup dry white wine
7 cups water

THE STEW

1 tablespoon butter
2 tablespoons water
1 quart mussels
½ cup water
1 cup minced leeks
1 cup diced potatoes
½ cup chopped onion
⅓ cup butter
2 tablespoons oil
1 cup boiling water
Salt and pepper
1 cup heavy cream
3 egg yolks

Have the fish man open the clams and save the juice. Ask him for the fish trimming: bones, heads, and skin. Shell the shrimp. Put the shrimp shells with all the other stock ingredients in a large kettle, cover, and cook 30 minutes. Strain the stock. Put 1 tablespoon of butter and 2 tablespoons of water in the top of a double boiler and cook the shrimp for 1½ minutes over simmering water. Turn off the heat and leave them to keep warm. Soak the mussels in cold water, then scrub with a stiff brush to remove moss and grit. Steam them in ½ cup water 2 or 3 minutes until they open. Shell them over the water to save their juice, discard the shells, add the mussels to the shrimp, and put the juice and water into the stock. Sauté the 3 vegetables in the ⅓ cup butter and the oil until they begin to soften. Add the boiling water and cook them until tender, season them, and add them and their water to the stock. Strain the clam juice and clams with the shrimp and mussels. Cook a minute over simmering water just to reheat them. Boil up the fish stock. Scald the cream, stir it into the egg yolks, and whisk into the soup. Do not boil again. Distribute the seafood in hot wide soup plates and pour the soup over it. *Serves 8*

Chinese Shrimp Soup

CHICKEN AND PORK CONSOMMÉ

2 pounds chicken soup parts
2 pounds spareribs, cut in pieces
Soup vegetables
2½ quarts water
Salt

THE SOUP

⅓ cup vermicelli
1½ cups bamboo shoots, or bean
   sprouts, washed and drained

1 cup watercress, steamed and
   chopped
2 tablespoons butter
½ pound fresh shrimp
Cubes of soybean cake
12 fresh water chestnuts, peeled and
   sliced

ACCOMPANIMENT

Soy sauce (optional)

Make the consommé the day before, because every bit of fat must be removed. Put all the consommé ingredients except the salt in a large kettle, bring to a boil, and simmer 30 minutes. Add salt to taste, and continue cooking another 30 minutes. Strain. Chill overnight and remove all the fat from the top. Cook the vermicelli in 8 cups of the consommé 10 minutes, then add the bamboo shoots or sprouts and cook 5 minutes more. Soften the watercress in the butter 2 minutes and add it. Cook the shrimp in ½ cup of water 1½ minutes, shell, cut each shrimp in half lengthwise, and add to the soup. Add small cubes of soybean cake and the water chestnuts (neither needs cooking). These additions are available in Chinese grocery shops; they thicken the soup. Pass soy sauce to stir in the soup if you like the salty taste. *Serves 8*

Soupe de Moules *(Mussel Soup)*
Les Frères Troisgros, Roanne

A visit to Roanne to dine chez Pierre et Jean Troisgros is a very rich experience. There is no greater food to be found in France. Their late and beloved father was a restaurateur and they took their turn under Fernand Point at Vienne, so they have always lived with great food and its preparation.

FISH STOCK

Fish trimmings
2 eel steaks
1 pound rockfish or fresh cod
1 onion, minced
1 teaspoon thyme
1 carrot, sliced
Salt and freshly ground pepper
10 cups water

MIREPOIX

6 ounces grated carrots
2 large onions, chopped fine
2 cloves garlic, crushed
5 tomatoes, skinned and sliced
1 tablespoon saffron
White part of 3 leeks, sliced
⅓ cup olive oil

THE SOUP

4 quarts mussels	1 cup heavy cream
3 shallots, minced	Pinch thyme
1 cup dry white wine	Salt and pepper

Put all the stock ingredients in a big kettle, cover, and cook 30 minutes. Strain the broth and reserve it; you should have 2 quarts. Meanwhile cook the ingredients of the mirepoix over low heat for 5 minutes, stirring so that it does not burn. Add the mirepoix to the strained fish stock and simmer it 40 minutes, covered. Soak the mussels 1 hour in cold water, discarding any broken shells. The mussels must be closed. Scrub and rinse them well so there will be no grit. Put the mussels, shallots, and wine in a large kettle, cover, and cook 2½ to 3 minutes until the mussels open; shake the pot a few times. Shell the mussels over the pot so all the juices will be saved. Discard the shells, and put the mussels back in their cooking liquid. When ready to serve, divide the mussels among hot soup plates and put their cooking liquid into the soup. Boil the cream with the thyme, add to the soup, check the seasoning, and pour the boiling soup over the mussels. Serves 8

Italian Shellfish Soup

1 pound fresh shrimp	THE SOUP
	2 quarts mussels
FISH STOCK	4 tablespoons olive oil
Fish trimmings	2 tablespoons butter
Shrimp shells	2 cloves garlic, crushed
½ cup chopped onions	1 leek, sliced fine
1 teaspoon thyme	1 cup dry white wine
1 pint clam juice	½ teaspoon each thyme and
4 cups water	marjoram
Salt and pepper	¼ cup tomato purée

Ask the fish man to give you some fish trimmings for the stock. Shell the shrimp and reserve. Add the shells to the trimmings and the rest of the ingredients for the stock (except the seasoning) in a large kettle. Cover and cook 25 minutes. Add the seasoning. Strain the stock. Soak the mussels 1 hour in cold water, then scrub them hard with a rough vegetable brush to remove all the moss and grit. Rinse well. Put the olive oil, butter, garlic, and leek in a big kettle and cook 2 minutes, then add the wine and the mussels. Cover and cook over medium heat until the mussels open—about 2 or 3 minutes. Shell the mussels over the pot to save all the juices. Put the mussels aside and discard the shells. Cook the shrimp in this liquid 1 minute, scoop them out, and add them to the mussels. Add the herbs and tomato purée to the cooking liquid and add the strained fish stock. When ready to serve bring the soup to a boil and add it to the mussels and shrimp. Serve in hot wide soup plates. *Serves 6*

VARIATION: Scald 1 cup heavy cream, mix it with 2 egg yolks, and whisk into the soup just before the seafood is added.

Mouclade *(Bordeaux Mussel Soup)*
Restaurant Oliver, Langon, France

Chef Marcel Berthe's fragrant mussel soup was a specialty of this lovely provincial hotel southeast of Bordeaux. We were driven down by M. Paul de Riviére, an old friend of the patronne, Madame Cécile Oliver who gave him and others shelter during the Resistance. She presented me with a copy of *Les Grands Vins de Bordeaux*, in which she inscribed "á Madame Stella Standard avec toute ma sympathie, C. Oliver, la mère de Raymond."

48 mussels	1 cup dry vermouth
3 tablespoons butter	3 tablespoons cornstarch
1 white onion, minced	2 teaspoons curry powder
1 large clove garlic, minced	Salt and freshly ground pepper
1 pint fish stock or clam juice	1 cup heavy cream

Soak the mussels an hour in cold water, then scrub them with a coarse vegetable brush to remove all the moss and grit. Rinse them well. Put the butter in a heavy pot with the onion and cook a moment, then add the garlic and liquids. Put the mussels on top, cover, and cook 2 or 3 minutes until the mussels open. Remove the top shells over the pot to save the juices, discard the top shells, and put the mussels on the half-shell in another pot and reserve. This may be done a little ahead of time. When ready to serve, reheat the soup. Mix the cornstarch, curry powder, and seasonings together and blend in the cream. When the mixture is smooth add it to the soup and cook it until thickened. Pour the boiling soup over the mussels and when they are hot, divide the mussels among wide soup plates and divide the soup over them. This is enough curry; it should not dominate the flavor but just "perfume" it. *Serves 6*

Moules Normande *(Normandy Mussel Soup)*

48 mussels	Salt and freshly ground pepper
3 cups clam juice	½ cup calvados (applejack)
¼ cup shredded carrots	¼ cup sweet butter
½ cup finely minced white onions	2 tablespoons cornstarch
1 teaspoon thyme	1½ cups heavy cream

Soak the mussels an hour in cold water, then scrub with a stiff brush to remove all moss and grit. Rinse them well. The vegetables must be very finely minced or shredded as the soup is not strained. Put 1 cup of the clam juice in a kettle with the vegetables and thyme, then add the mussels. Cover and cook 2 minutes or until the mussels open. Remove the top shells over the kettle to save all the juices and put the mussels on the half-shell into a bowl. Put the additional 2 cups of clam juice in the kettle, with the salt, pepper, calvados, and butter. Cover and simmer gently 3 minutes. Blend the cornstarch with the cream, add to the soup, and cook until thickened. Divide the mussels among hot soup plates and divide the boiling soup over them. *Serves 6*

Mussel and Clam Soup

For inland people who find it hard to get fresh clams and mussels.

2 tablespoons butter	1 9-ounce can Danish Bonavita
1 white onion, minced	Limfjord mussels
¼ cup grated carrot	1 cup heavy cream
3 cloves garlic, crushed	3 tablespoons cornstarch
4 shallots, minced	Salt and pepper
½ teaspoon thyme	2 teaspoons curry powder
1 pint clam juice	1 can minced clams
1 cup dry vermouth	

Put the butter, onion, and carrot in a large saucepan and cook about 30 seconds, then add the garlic, shallots, thyme, clam juice, and vermouth. Drain the juice from the can of mussels and add. Cover and boil 5 minutes. This may stand in a crockery or enamel bowl. When ready to serve, blend the cream with the cornstarch and seasonings. Reheat the soup, add the cream mixture, bring to the boil, and cook until thickened. Add the mussels and minced clams, reheat, and serve. Seafood must not be overcooked so it is added just before serving. *Serves 6*

Potage de Moules *(Cream of Mussels Soup)*

3 quarts mussels	2½ tablespoons cornstarch
1 onion, minced	4 cups strained fish stock
1 stalk celery, minced fine	Salt and freshly ground pepper
1 clove garlic, crushed	¼ teaspoon nutmeg
1 cup clam juice	¼ cup Pernod
1¾ cups dry white wine	1 cup heavy cream

Soak, scrub, and rinse the mussels. Put the onion, celery, garlic, clam juice, and 1 cup of the wine in a kettle and lay the mussels on top. Cover and steam 2 minutes or until the mussels open. Shell the mussels over the kettle to save their juices; set the mussels aside. Mix the remaining ¾ cup of wine with the cornstarch until smooth, then add the fish stock. Add the mixture to the kettle in which the mussels cooked, add seasonings and simmer 5 minutes. When ready to serve, reheat and add the Pernod and cream. When the soup is hot, add the mussels. *Serves 8*

Les Escrevisses Cardinalisees au Champagne
(Crayfish or lobster tails with Champagne)
François Minot, Hôtel de la Côte-d'Or, Saulieu

M. Minot says: "This recipe is *grande cuisine* but simple at the same time. It is an ideal preparation for appreciating the finesse and the delicate taste of these charming crustaceans." M. Minot, who succeeded Alexandre Dumaine, has kept this restaurant one of the culinary ornaments of France. All the classic dishes are here and all the great Burgundies.

24 fine good-sized crayfish, or 4 lobster tails	1 teaspoon thyme
	2 bay leaves
	2 tablespoons minced parsley
COURT BOUILLON	1 teaspoon chervil
	Rind of 1 lemon, grated
1 bottle dry champagne	Salt, pepper, cayenne
1 quart water	
⅓ cup *fine champagne* (brandy)	
⅓ cup each minced shallots, onion, and carrots	GARNISH
2 cloves garlic, crushed	Sprigs of parsley

This is such a great idea that I have made the soup with lobster tails since crayfish are hard to find. If you can get crayfish, soak them 24 hours in fresh water. Put all the ingredients for the *court bouillon* in a large kettle, partly cover, and simmer 45 minutes to reduce. Remove the crayfish from the soaking water and wash and rinse them well. Put them in the simmering bouillon and cook 12 minutes. Remove the kettle from the heat and let stand 5 minutes. Divide the crayfish on heated plates and serve the bouillon in cups at the same time, garnishing each cup with parsley.

Lobster tails should cook in the bouillon 15 to 18 minutes, depending on their size. With lobster tails, I suggest serving melted butter or mayonnaise. Serve the bouillon in cups. *Serves 4*

Dried Legume Soups

Preparing Dried Legumes for Soups

Soups containing dried peas, beans, or lentils have been grouped in this chapter, because the cook must remember that these require soaking several hours or overnight before the soup is started. When salt pork is used, any additional salt is added when the soup is done.

Baked Pea or Bean Soup

1½ cups dried split peas or white beans	2 teaspoons marjoram
4 cups water	2 teaspoons chervil
4 ounces salt pork, sliced and diced	Salt and pepper
2 pounds or more fresh pork butt or breast of veal	½ cup chopped onions
2 tablespoons flour	½ cup chopped carrots
	8 cups hot chicken stock

Wash the peas or beans. Soak the peas in the water 4 or 5 hours. If beans are used, soak overnight. The beans are covered and simmered 45 minutes or until they are tender. The peas do not need preliminary cooking. Put the diced salt pork in a casserole and fry it until it is golden. Cut the meat in 2-inch cubes if it is to be served separately; much smaller, if served in the soup. Shake the cubes in the pork fat until golden, then add the onions and carrots. Stir a few minutes, then add the peas or beans with their liquid. Mix with the meat and vegetables and add the hot stock. Cover and cook in a 300° oven for 2 hours. Add a little boiling water if necessary to keep a soup consistency. When the meat is tender the soup is done. This is a flexible soup, and more or less meat may be used. *Two pounds of meat will serve 6*

VARIATION: Bean and Celeriac Soup. Peel a good-sized celery root, dice it fine, and add it to the other vegetables. *Makes 2½ quarts*

Basque Vegetable Soup

1 cup dried beans	2 cloves garlic, crushed
4 cups water	Salt and freshly ground pepper
1 cup chopped onions	1 teaspoon oregano
1/3 cup butter or ham fat	3 tablespoons wine vinegar
Half a new cabbage, shredded fine	4 to 6 cups boiling water

Wash and soak the beans in the water overnight. Simmer the beans 1 hour. Soften the onions in the butter or ham fat until golden, then add them to the beans along with the shredded cabbage and the garlic. Add salt, pepper, herb and vinegar. Add 4 to 6 cups boiling water and cook gently, covered for 1 hour. Check seasoning. When using water in soups the flavor may be improved by adding 2 teaspoons of chicken soup concentrate. *Serves 6 to 8*

Bean Soup with Roast Meat Bones

1½ cups dried beans: black, white, kidney, lima, pinto, or northern
4 cups water

STOCK

Bones from roast beef, lamb, pork, game, or poultry
4 stalks celery, sliced
2 carrots, sliced
2 large onions, sliced
2 teaspoons thyme
2 teaspoons marjoram
Salt and pepper

Leftover poultry stuffing, if available
1 teaspoon beef or chicken extract
6 cups water (or water and juices)
Leftover gravy, if available

THE SOUP
1 large onion, diced
1 thick slice salt pork, cut in 1-inch cubes
1 teaspoon mustard
2 or 3 tablespoons molasses
2 tablespoons tomato paste
1 tablespoon vinegar

Wash the beans and soak in 4 cups of water overnight. Put all the stock ingredients except the extract and the gravy in a larger kettle. Cover with 6 cups liquid, part of which may be a can of vegetable juice and a can of carrot juice. Cover and simmer gently 1½ hours, then strain it and stir in the extract and gravy. To cook the beans, add enough water to make a quart and add the onion, cubes of pork, and all the seasonings. Cover and simmer until the beans are tender, 1 to 1½ hours; limas take less time than the others. If necessary, add more boiling water. Remove 1 cup of beans and purée them to thicken the soup. Check the beans for salt and pepper. Mix the beans and the purée with the stock. Serve the soup in cups and serve the cubes of pork on bread or crackers as an accompaniment. This is a fine soup with or without the beans. Bones make a marvelous soup; they should never be discarded without first making soup. *Serves 10 to 12*

Black Bean Soup

2 cups dried black beans
4 cups water
½ pound salt pork
¾ pound ground round of beef, or a
    ham bone with meat on it
3 quarts water
2 good-sized onions, diced
2 carrots, diced
2 stalks celery, sliced thin
2 teaspoons basil
2 whole cloves

1½ tablespoons molasses
1 teaspoon mustard
½ teaspoon mace
2 teaspoons salt
Freshly ground pepper
Dash cayenne
½ cup Madeira or sherry

GARNISH

Lemon slices
Sieved hard-cooked egg

Wash the beans well and soak them overnight in 4 cups water. Drain, measure the water, and add enough to make 3 quarts. Put the beans, water, salt pork, and ground beef or ham bone in a large kettle, bring to a boil, and skim. Add all the vegetables and seasonings except the salt, pepper, cayenne, and Madeira. Cover and simmer very gently 3 hours. Add a little boiling water if needed. When the soup is done, remove the ham bone, if used, and purée the soup. A blender produces a fine creamy texture. Season with salt, pepper, and cayenne. Before serving, reheat the soup, then add the wine. Put a thin slice of lemon and some sieved hard-cooked egg over the top of each plate of soup. This is an elegant soup for family as well as for important dinners. *Serves 10*

Chickpea Soup

1½ cups dried chickpeas
4 cups water
2 pounds neck of lamb (in one
    piece)
1 cup diced onions
2 tablespoons minced parsley
½ teaspoon ginger
1 teaspoon turmeric

5 cups warm water
4 chicken legs
4 chicken thighs
⅓ cup Patna rice
½ cup tomato purée
2 teaspoons coriander
Salt and pepper

Wash the chickpeas and soak them overnight in 4 cups of water. Do not drain the peas but put them in a soup kettle with the lamb, onions, seasonings, and 5 cups of warm water. Bring to the boil and skim. Cover and cook gently 2 hours. Add the chicken pieces, the rice, and the rest of the ingredients. Cover and cook slowly 30 minutes, or until the chicken is tender. Serve the soup first in bowls. Keep the lamb and chicken warm and serve as the next course with a vegetable and a fruit chutney. *Serves 6 to 8*

Chickpea Soup with Peanuts

2 cups dried chickpeas
1 cup chopped onions
2 leeks, sliced
4 tablespoons butter
1 carrot, diced
1 pound streaky salt pork (in 1 piece)

2½ quarts chicken stock, or 2½ quarts water plus 2 tablespoons chicken soup concentrate
Salt and pepper
⅓ cup ground peanuts or peanut butter

Wash the chickpeas and soak them overnight in 1 quart of water; do not drain. Boil up the pork and drain it. When making the soup, soften the onions and leeks in the butter in the bottom of a soup kettle, add the carrot, the peas and their liquid, the pork, and the chicken stock or water and soup concentrate. Cover and cook gently 2 to 2½ hours, or until the pork is tender. Remove the pork. Take out 2 cups of peas, purée the rest of the soup, and then return the peas to it. Check the seasoning for salt and pepper. Stir in the ground peanuts or peanut butter. The peanut butter makes a smooth, nutty soup; more may be added to taste. *Serves 10 or more*

Sopa de Garbanzo *(Spinach and Chickpea Soup)*

2 cups chickpeas
2½ quarts water
2 ounces salt pork, diced
2 tablespoons butter or oil
1 cup finely diced onions
1 cup finely diced carrots
2 cloves garlic, crushed
Salt and pepper

⅓ cup tomato purée
1 pound fresh spinach
1 teaspoon oregano
1 cup water

GARNISH

4 or 5 Spanish sausages, fried and sliced

Wash the chickpeas and soak them in a soup kettle overnight in 2½ quarts water. Fry the salt pork in the butter or oil until crisp, then scoop the pieces out and reserve them. Fry the onions in the fat until they color, then scrape them into the kettle along with the carrots and garlic. Cover and simmer gently 1 hour. Add salt, pepper, and tomato purée and cook another hour. If the soup becomes very thick add some boiling water. Meanwhile, wash and trim the spinach. Cook it in a separate pot with the oregano and water until tender, then purée it with its juices. Purée 2 cups of the soup and return it to the kettle, adding the spinach purée and the diced pork. Reheat the soup. Sauté the sausages and slice them. Put three slices in each soup plate, and pour the soup over them. *Serves 10*

Bean Soup with Fresh Herbs

1½ cups white, northern, or navy
  beans
2 quarts water
1 large potato, diced
½ cup diced onions
1 small carrot, diced
1 teaspoon thyme
Salt and pepper

1 quart water
1 cup closely packed sorrel or
  watercress
⅓ cup parsley
2 large lettuce leaves
3 tablespoons minced fresh herbs:
  tarragon, thyme, chervil
4 or 5 tablespoons butter

Wash the beans and soak overnight in the water. To make the soup, add the vegetables, 1 teaspoon thyme, salt, pepper, and another quart of water. Cover and simmer 1½ hours or until the beans are tender. Purée half the soup and return it to the rest of the soup. Puréeing soups in this way makes a creamy texture instead of a watery soup.

Put all the herbs in a wooden bowl and chop them very fine. Do not grind them. Heat the butter and soften them in it 2 or 3 minutes. They may be covered to prevent burning but should be stirred occasionally. Add them to the soup and cook about 3 minutes. If the soup is thicker than heavy cream, thin it with a little boiling water. *Serves 8 to 10*

Lentil Soup

2 cups dried lentils
4 cups water
Bones of roast beef, lamb, or pork
2 large onions, chopped fine
2 carrots, chopped fine
2 stalks celery, sliced, with leaves
2 teaspoons oregano
2 teaspoons salt
¼ teaspoon powdered clove

2 bay leaves
Freshly ground pepper
3 tablespoons lime juice, or ⅓ cup
    Madeira or sherry

GARNISH

Knackwurst, sliced and spread with
    mustard

Pick over the lentils and wash thoroughly. Soak them in the water 4 or 5 hours. Put them in the soup kettle with all the other ingredients except the lime juice or wine. Cover and simmer gently 2 hours, then remove the bones and bay leaves. Remove 1 cup lentils. Purée the rest of the soup. Return the whole lentils to the purée and add the juice or wine. Boil the knackwurst 10 minutes, skin, and cut in slices. Spread the slices with mustard and put 3 slices in each soup plate. *Makes 2 quarts*

Game Soup with Lentils

1 cup lentils
3 cups water
2 whole cloves garlic
2 bay leaves
3½ cups chicken stock
Salt and pepper

GAME BROTH

Carcass and leftover meat of game:
    quail, duck, goose, partridge
Stuffing and gravy, if available
1 onion stuck with 3 cloves

1 onion, sliced
1 sliced carrot
4 cups beef or chicken stock
1 cup red wine
6 crushed juniper berries
1 teaspoon each thyme and sage
Water to cover

GARNISH

4 or 5 chicken livers
2 tablespoons butter
½ cup Madeira

Wash the lentils well and soak 6 hours or overnight in 3 cups of water. Drain them and cook them with the garlic, bay leaves, and chicken stock 1 hour, covered. Season with salt and pepper and set aside. To make the game broth, put the game carcasses in a large kettle with all the other ingredients. (Game too old and tough to eat also makes excellent soup.) Cover and simmer gently 1½ hours. Strain and add the lentils and their liquid. Cut the chicken livers in pieces, brown them lightly in the butter, and purée them with 1 cup of the broth and lentils. Add to the soup. Before serving, reheat the soup and add the Madeira. Serve in soup plates.

VARIATION: Scald ¾ cup heavy cream, pour it over 2 egg yolks, and whisk into the soup. If desired, put 2 tablespoons Madeira in each soup plate before adding the soup. *Serves 8*

Habitant Pea Soup
Château Frontenac, Quebec

2 cups dried yellow peas	½ cup celery tops
8 cups water	1 teaspoon basil
½ pound salt pork (in one piece)	1 teaspoon savory
3 carrots, diced	Pepper
3 onions, diced	Salt
2 white turnips, peeled and diced	

Wash the peas and soak them overnight in the water. Before making the soup, measure the water and add enough to make 2½ quarts. Put the water and peas in a soup kettle, add the pork, bring to a boil, and skim. Add the vegetables and the seasonings with the exception of the salt. Cover and simmer gently 2 hours, add salt, and cook 1 more hour. Remove the pork and 1 cup of peas. Put the soup through a sieve or purée in a blender. Return the peas to the soup. Slice the pork and put a slice in each bowl of soup. *Serves 8*

Near East Lentil Soup

2 cups lentils	1 cup closely packed spinach
4 cups water	2 tablespoons lime juice
1¼ cups chopped onions	
4 tablespoons olive oil	ACCOMPANIMENT
4 cups chicken broth	Croutons fried in olive oil with
2 whole cloves garlic	crushed garlic
Salt and pepper	

Wash and pick over the lentils and rinse them well. Soak them 6 hours or overnight in the water. Sauté the onions in the olive oil in the bottom of a soup kettle until golden, then add the lentils and their soaking water, the broth, garlic, and seasonings. Cover and simmer gently 1¼ hours. Chop the spinach quite fine in a wooden bowl, add it to the lentils, and simmer 20 minutes more. Add the lime juice. Serve the soup in bowls, accompanied by a bowl of croutons. *Serves 6 or more*

North African Soup *(Lamb and Chickpea Soup)*

This is really a United Nations Soup, as a Hollander gave this North African soup to an American at the home of a Spaniard in Paris.

2 cups chickpeas
2 quarts water
2 pounds neck of lamb, cubed
3 tablespoons oil
½ pound onions, minced
2½ pounds tomatoes, skinned and
    sliced, or 2 cups tomato purée

Salt and pepper
2 teaspoons savory
1 tablespoon sweet paprika
2 small zucchini, sliced
½ cup vermicelli

Wash the chickpeas and soak them 6 hours in the water in the bottom of a soup kettle. Brown the lamb cubes in the oil until golden. Stir in the onion, cook a few seconds, then scrape into the soup kettle and add the peas. Add the tomatoes or tomato purée and the seasonings. Cover and simmer 2 hours. Add hot water if the soup is too thick. Add the zucchini, cook 10 minutes more. This is a thick and nourishing soup. *Serves 8 or more*

Pepé's Caldo Gallego *(Pepé's Bean Soup)*
Galicia, Spain

1½ cups dried white beans or lima
    beans, or a mixture of the two
1 quart water
1 or 2 6-ounce chunks pork belly
2 quarts water, or part water and
    part meat or poultry broth
½ cup finely diced onions
1 big potato, finely cubed

Half a new cabbage, finely shredded
Salt and pepper
½ pound browned pork sausages
    (optional)

ACCOMPANIMENT

Dijon mustard

Wash the beans and soak them in the water 6 hours or overnight. Do not drain. Add 4 more cups of water and put in a soup kettle, and add the pork, liquid, onions, and potato. Cover and simmer gently 1¾ hours. Add the cabbage and cook 45 minutes more or until the pork is very tender. Add salt and pepper. Brown the sausages (if used) and cook them 15 minutes, then add them to the soup for the last 5 minutes. Remove the pork and sausages, put them on a hot platter, and serve with mustard. Serve the soup in bowls at the same time. This is a very good peasant soup. *Makes about 2½ quarts*

Lima Bean Soup

1½ cups dried lima beans	Salt and pepper
1 quart water	3 cloves garlic
1 cup chopped onions	1 teaspoon chervil
1 cup chopped carrots	1 teaspoon marjoram
1 cup finely sliced celery	¼ cup minced parsley
2 leeks, sliced	1 cup light cream (optional)
2 shallots, minced	
1 white turnip, peeled and diced	GARNISH
1 parsnip, diced	1 pound fresh lima or peas, cooked

Wash the beans and soak them in the water 6 hours or overnight. Do not drain. Add 4 more cups of water and put in a soup kettle with all the other ingredients except the cream. Cover and simmer gently 1½ hours, or until the beans are soft. If the soup is too thick add a little boiling water while cooking. Purée the contents of the pot. Add the cream if desired. Using limas as a garnish is most appropriate to lima bean soup but they are not always in the market, so peas may be used instead. Cook the limas or peas in 3 tablespoons butter and ⅓ cup water until tender and add them and the liquid to the soup. Check for seasoning. *Makes 2 quarts or more*

Greek Lamb and Split-Pea Soup

1 cup dried green split peas	½ cup chopped onions
1 quart water	½ cup tomato purée
2½ pounds neck of lamb, with bone	2 quarts chicken stock, or 2 quarts
2 tablespoons flour	water and 2 tablespoons chicken
Salt and pepper	soup concentrate
2 teaspoons oregano	Pepper
¼ cup olive oil	Salt
1 cup diced carrots	½ cup Patna rice
1 leek, sliced	Chopped parsley
1 white turnip, peeled and diced	

Wash the split peas and soak them in the water 4 or 5 hours. Cut the lamb into small cubes. Put the flour, salt, pepper, and 1 teaspoon of the oregano in paper bag and shake the cubes of lamb in it until well covered. Brown the lamb in the oil until golden on all sides, then add it and the bone to the peas, with the rest of the oregano and all the other ingredients except the salt, rice, and parsley. Cover, cook 1 hour, add salt and cook 1 hour more. Add the rice and cook 30 minutes longer. Remove the lamb bone. Take out 2 cups of the soup and vegetables, purée, and return to the soup. Add the parsley. *Serves 8 or more*

Soupe Auvergnate *(Lentil Soup of Auvergne)*

1 pound slice pork butt
1 cup lentils
2 cups water
1 pound potatoes, peeled and diced
4 large leeks, sliced
1 clove garlic, crushed
2 teaspoons thyme
Pepper

2 tablespoons butter
1 cup shredded cabbage
2 quarts water
Salt

GARNISH

½ cup minced fresh herbs: parsley, tarragon, chives, or chervil

Cut the pork into small cubes. Wash and pick over the lentils and rinse them well. Soak them 6 hours or overnight in the 2 cups water. Put all the ingredients except the salt and garnish into the soup kettle. Cover and simmer for 2 hours. Add salt after it has cooked 1 hour. Take out 2 cups of soup, purée, and return to the kettle. Reheat soup before serving and sprinkle each plate of soup with 1 or 2 teaspoons of the fresh herbs. *Serves 6 to 8*

Soupe Haricot Rouge *(Red Bean Soup)*

2 cups dried red beans or kidney beans
1 quart water
1 cup chopped onions
1 tablespoon prepared mustard
½ cup thinly sliced celery
½ cup diced carrots
1 cup dry red wine

2 tablespoons brown sugar
1½-inch slice salt pork, diced
Salt and pepper
6 cups water
3 tablespoons chopped parsley

GARNISH

Croutons fried in butter

Wash the beans and soak them overnight in 1 quart of water. Put the beans and their soaking water in a soup kettle and add all the other ingredients except the parsley. Add 6 more cups of water. Cover and cook 2 hours or until the beans are soft. Take out 1 cup of beans, purée the rest of the soup, and return the 1 cup beans to the purée. Add the parsley. If the soup is too thick, water, broth, or wine may be added. The consistency should be like heavy cream. Serve with a bowl of crisp croutons. *Serves 10*

Pasta e Fagioli *(Pasta and Bean Soup)*
Rosteria Luciano, Bologna

This restaurant is run by our great friends Luciano and Maria Dragnetti. Maria has received many honors for her cooking. They are a friendly and engaging couple and give everyone a warm welcome and a wonderful meal. Luciano has a fine wine cellar which contains all the great French Burgundies and Bordeaux, as well as the fine wines from the vineyard of Signor Negroni near Bologna, which produces some of the finest red and white wines in Italy.

2 cups dried lima beans, or 1½ pounds fresh or dried broad beans	Salt and pepper
	2 large tomatoes, peeled and sliced
1 slice salt pork or 1 strip bacon, diced	2 large potatoes, peeled and diced
	2 quarts water
3 tablespoons olive oil	4 ounces pasta in mixed shapes, or ¾ cup cooked rice
2 cloves garlic, crushed	
3 tablespoons minced parsley	

This is a thick and nourishing soup, especially good for winter and for a number of people. If dried limas are used, wash them and soak them 6 hours or overnight in 4 cups of water. Cook the diced salt pork or bacon in the olive oil until the pieces are golden, then scoop them out and reserve them. Add the garlic, parsley, salt, pepper, and tomatoes to the oil and cook slowly about 10 minutes, then reserve. If fresh broad beans are used cook them with the potatoes in 2 quarts of water 2 hours; add salt and pepper after 1 hour. With dried broad beans, add the potatoes and the 2 quarts of water to the beans and simmer gently 3 hours. Put them through a sieve or purée in a blender. If the soup is too thick add a little boiling water. Cook the pasta separately, drain, and add to the soup. If cooked rice is used, stir it into the soup and the reserved tomato mixture and diced pork or bacon. *Makes over 2 quarts*

Spanish Pork-and-Bean Soup

1½ cups white beans	6 white onions
2½ quarts water	6 young carrots
2 pounds pickled pork butt	6 small parsnips, scraped
2 leeks, sliced	6 potatoes
1 cup chopped onions	1 small new cabbage, cut in sixths
Bouquet garni: parsley, thyme, and tarragon	
	ACCOMPANIMENTS
Salt and pepper	Mustard
6 small white turnips, peeled	Black bread

Wash the beans and soak them in a soup kettle overnight. Two hours and a quarter before serving, put the pork in the kettle along with the leeks, chopped onions, and bouquet garni, and cook, covered, 1¾ hours. Add salt and pepper. Lay all the whole vegetables on top, cover, and cook 30 minutes. Drain out the whole vegetables and the pork. Slice the pork. Serve the meat and vegetables on a hot platter and serve the soup in bowls at the same time. *Serves 6 or more*

Split-Pea Soup with Greens

2 cups split peas
1 quart water
1 slice salt pork, diced
4 strips bacon, diced
2 tablespoons butter
2 leeks, sliced
2 cups chopped onions
1 carrot, diced
1 small celery root, diced
2 teaspoons basil

2 tablespoons minced parsley
1 potato, diced
Salt and pepper
2 teaspoons chicken soup concentrate
2 cups lettuce, sorrel, or spinach chopped or shredded fine
½ cup tiny egg noodles, cooked and drained (optional)

Wash the peas and soak them 6 hours in the water. Fry the diced salt pork and bacon in the butter in a soup kettle until crisp, then scoop out the pieces and reserve. Put the leeks and onions in the butter and stir and cook them until they soften, then add the peas and their soaking water, the carrot, celery root, basil, parsley, and potato. Cover and cook slowly 1 hour, then add salt and pepper and soup concentrate. At this point half of the soup may be puréed, if desired, and then returned to the soup kettle. Add more boiling water if soup is too thick. Add the greens and cook 5 minutes. If you wish to extend the soup add the cooked noodle shells. This is a fine nourishing soup. *Makes over 2 quarts*

Erwtensoep *(Dutch Split-Pea Soup)*

1 ham bone with meat
2 cups split peas
1 quart water
1 large celery root, chopped fine
4 leeks, chopped fine
2 cups finely minced onion
1 teaspoon basil
1 teaspoon thyme
Salt and pepper
2 quarts water

2 fresh pig knuckles or pig's feet
2 pickled pig knuckles or pig's feet
12 pork sausages

ACCOMPANIMENTS

Fried croutons
Mashed potatoes
Dijon mustard
Dutch beer

This is a meal in itself. If you plan to serve 8, get a ham bone with plenty of meat on it. Wash the peas well and soak them 3 or 4 hours in 1 quart water. Do not drain them. Chop and mince the vegetables very fine because this soup is not puréed and it should be creamy and smooth. Put the peas and the soaking water in a large soup kettle with the vegetables, herbs, salt and pepper. Cover and cook 20 minutes. Add the meats, except the sausages, cover, and cook 2½ to 3 hours or until the meats are tender. Add more boiling water when necessary. Brown the sausages quickly without cooking them and add them 20 minutes before the soup is done. Drain the meats from the soup and put them on a hot platter. Serve the soup with a tureen; sprinkle croutons over the top. Serve the soup in bowls at the same time you serve the meat. Serve mashed potatoes and Dijon mustard with the meats, with Dutch beer as a beverage. *Serves 4 to 6*

Cream of Split Pea Soup

2 cups dried split peas	Salt and pepper
1 quart water	3 or 4 cups water
1 large onion, sliced	Milk or half-and-half
3 tablespoons butter	
1 cup sliced carrots	GARNISH (optional)
1 ham bone, or bone from roast lamb or pork	1 pound fresh peas cooked in 2 tablespoons butter with 2
2 bay leaves	teaspoons basil, salt, and pepper

Wash the peas and soak them 5 or 6 hours in the water. Soften the onion in a soup kettle with the butter, then add the peas and the soaking water, carrots, bone, bay leaves, salt, pepper, and 3 or 4 cups of water. Cover and simmer 1¼ hours. If soup is too thick, add a little boiling water. Remove the bone and the bay leaves and purée the soup. Add enough milk or half-and-half to make a consistency of heavy cream. The garnish is optional but it makes a nice addition, especially if the soup is for guests. Cook the peas in the butter and as little water as possible, add salt, pepper and basil. Add the peas and liquid to the soup. Check for seasoning. *Serves 8 or more in soup cups*

Swedish Pea Soup

2 cups dried yellow peas
3 quarts water
1 onion stuck with 3 cloves
1 cup diced onions
2 leeks, sliced
2 carrots, thinly sliced
2 teaspoons chervil
2 teaspoons basil
½ pound bacon (in one piece)

6 ounces streaky salt pork
2 pounds fresh pork butt
Salt and freshly ground pepper
¾ teaspoon ginger
Juice of ½ lemon

ACCOMPANIMENTS

Black bread
Mustard

Wash the peas and soak them 6 hours or overnight in the water in a soup kettle. To make the soup add all the other ingredients, cover, and cook 2 hours or until the meats are tender. Purée half the soup and combine with the rest. Add more boiling water if it is too thick. Check the seasoning. Serve the soup in bowls and serve the meats at the same time or as a separate course; put them on a platter and carve at the table. This is a complete meal. *Serves 8 to 10*

Theo's Snert *(Dutch Split Pea and Leek Soup)*

1 pound dried green split peas
2½ quarts water
3-ounce slice salt pork
1½ pounds leeks, sliced
1 stalk celery, chopped fine

1 celery root, finely diced
Salt and pepper
1 pound pork sausages
1½ pounds potatoes, peeled and
    diced fine

Wash the peas and soak them in the water 5 or 6 hours in a large kettle. Brown the pork and add it to the peas with the leeks, celery, celery root, salt, and pepper. Cover and cook 1½ hours. Brown the sausages quickly, add them and the potatoes, and cook 20 minutes more. If it is too thick add a little boiling water. If you like a creamier texture, remove 3 cups of the soup, purée it, and return it to the kettle. *Makes over 3 quarts*

Three-Bean Soup

1 cup navy beans	Salt and pepper
1 cup split beans	2 teaspoons thyme
1 cup black beans or lentils	2 teaspoons basil
4 quarts water	2 teaspoons chervil
½ pound streaky salt pork	½ teaspoon powdered clove
2 or 3 pounds breast of veal or fresh pork butt	1 pound pork sausage (optional)
2 cups finely chopped onions	ACCOMPANIMENTS
2 leeks, sliced	Croutons fried in butter
2 white turnips, peeled and diced	Dijon mustard
1 cup chopped carrots	

Wash all the legumes. If you use lentils, pick them over, wash, and rinse well. Put all three in a large soup kettle, add 2 quarts of the water, and soak overnight. Add the other 2 quarts of water, bring to a boil, and skim. Add the rest of the ingredients, cover, and simmer gently 2 hours or until the meats are tender. Don't add much salt when cooking with salt pork. The seasoning can be checked at the end. Purée half of the soup and return it to the kettle. Serve the meats separately with Dijon mustard and serve the soup in bowls. Sprinkle the top of each bowl of soup with croutons. This recipe makes enough soup for 12. If you wish to serve that number, another pound of meat is required. You can extend the meat with 1 pound pork sausages. Brown them quickly and add to the soup 20 minutes before it is done. *Serves 8 to 12*

Cereal, Cheese, Beer, Egg, Garlic, Pasta, Wine, and Yoghurt Soups

Cream of Barley Soup

½ cup barley
2 cups water
5 cups rich chicken or veal broth
1 cup heavy cream
2 egg yolks
Chopped parsley

GARNISHES

Cooked peas with basil
Liver or veal quenelles (see index)
Buttered croutons
Cooked asparagus tips

Soak the barley in the water 4 hours. Add the barley and soaking water to the broth and simmer 10 minutes. When ready to serve reheat the soup. Scald the cream, mix it with the egg yolks and whisk into the soup. Add chopped parsley. Add any one of the suggested garnishes to give interest to the soup. *Serves 6 to 8*

Macaroni in Brodo *(Macaroni Soup)*

This soup, popular in Italy, replaces the pasta course.

6 ounces elbow macaroni
Salted boiling water
3 tablespoons butter, melted
¼ cup grated Parmesan cheese
¼ cup minced parsley
6 or 8 cups boiling rich chicken,
    beef, or veal stock

GARNISH

Bowl of grated Parmesan or Gruyère
    cheese

Cook the macaroni in boiling salted water until tender, drain, and toss with the melted butter, Parmesan cheese, and parsley. Have the stock boiling and add the macaroni. Pass a bowl of cheese to sprinkle over the top. Rotelle is a very attractive pasta to use for this soup.

VARIATION: Add 1 cup tomato purée to the stock before adding the pasta; or add ½ cup of heavy cream with or without the tomato purée. Either will extend the soup. *Serves 6 to 8*

Italian Rice Soup

1/3 cup Italian or Patna rice
6 or 7 cups veal or chicken broth
1/3 cup finely diced onions
1/3 cup julienne sticks of carrots
2 eggs

1/4 cup grated Parmesan cheese
1/3 cup chopped parsley

GARNISH

Bowl of grated Parmesan cheese

Soak the rice in the broth several hours so it will cook more quickly. Add the vegetables to the broth and rice, cover, and cook slowly 20 minutes, or until the rice is done. If the soup is too thick, add a little more hot broth. Beat the eggs in the bottom of a warmed soup tureen until thick and stir in the cheese. Pour the boiling soup over them and add the parsley. *Serves 6 to 8, depending on the amount of broth*

Rice Soup with Liver Quenelles or Foie Gras

1 cup cooked Patna or brown rice
6 cups rich chicken consommé
2 or 3 teaspoons curry powder
Salt and pepper

GARNISH

Liver quenelles (see index), or tiny balls of pâté de foie gras

Leftover cooked rice can be used for this. Rice cooked in consommé is better than that cooked in water. In any case put half the cooked rice in a blender with 2 cups of the consommé and purée it until very smooth. Empty it into a saucepan and rinse the blender with another cup of consommé, then combine all with the purée. Stir in the curry powder and the rest of the rice. Check the seasoning for salt and pepper. Reheat to serve and garnish each plate of soup with 3 or 4 little liver quenelles or pâté de foie gras balls. This can easily be extended with more consommé, a little white wine, and/or heavy cream. To vary it, add a tablespoon of tomato paste. Some may like a good pinch of sugar with curry. *Serves 6 to 8*

Nebraska Cornmeal Soup

1 cup thinly sliced onions	¼ cup cornmeal
⅓ cup butter or ham fat	5 cups hot chicken stock
Salt and pepper	1 cup hot heavy cream

Sauté the onions in the butter or ham fat until they color, then add a little salt and pepper. (This can be done in the top of a double boiler.) Stir the cornmeal into the onions and slowly add the hot stock. Cover and cook 30 minutes over gently simmering water. Stir occasionally. Add the hot cream. *Serves 6*

Potage à l'Avoine *(Oats soup)*
Marc Chevillot, Hotel de la Poste, Beaune

Marc said that his mother made this soup for the children when he was young. He represents the third generation to preside over this lovely hotel. Beaune, in the center of the Burgundy wine country, is a delightful town to visit, especially during the *vendage*. Game is in season then and with the great Burgundy wines, a meal is an experience never to be forgotten.

⅓ cup butter	6 young carrots, diced
⅔ cup fine steel-cut oats	3 leeks, sliced
2 quarts boiling water	Salt

Melt the butter in a heavy pot, stir in the oats, and shake them over low heat until they are golden. Add the boiling water, vegetables, and salt. Cover and cook slowly 45 minutes. Stir occasionally. The consistency should be like cream, so if necessary add a little boiling water. Use unprocessed oats for a fine and nourishing dish. This is especially welcome in winter.

VARIATION: Use 1 cup coarse steel-cut oats browned in a heavy, dry pot. Add 3 cups boiling chicken broth. Then add the vegetables, diced very fine. Cover and cook 25 more minutes or longer. Serve instead of potatoes to accompany meat. *Serves 4 to 6*

Pearl Barley and Poultry Soup

Carcass of a chicken, duck, turkey, goose, or game bird
Leftover stuffing and gravy
Salt and pepper
1 cup chopped carrots
1 cup chopped celery and leaves
1 cup chopped onions
2 whole cloves
½ teaspoon thyme
1 teaspoon marjoram
1 white turnip, peeled and diced
1 parsnip, sliced
2½ to 3 quarts water
1 cup pearl barley

Disjoint the carcass and put it in the bottom of a large soup kettle. Add all the other ingredients except the barley. The water should cover the ingredients. Cover and cook 2 hours. Remove the bones and strain the soup. Add the barley to the strained soup and cook 15 minutes or until the soup is clear. If the soup is too thick add some broth. A cup of white wine may be added in the first cooking of the soup. Light cream may also be used to add to the soup. Soaked split peas may be used instead of barley. This is a flexible soup and a very nourishing one. *Makes well over 2 quarts*

Chinese Egg-Drop Soup

Chicken and pork consommé (see Chinese Shrimp Soup in index)
1 egg for each 2 cups of consommé

Have the consommé simmering. Beat the eggs and put them through a coarse sieve into the consommé. Stir and serve. The eggs cook immediately.

Egg Soup

½ cup minced onion
1 leek, sliced
⅓ cup olive oil
1 tomato, peeled and chopped
1 tablespoon tomato paste
4 cloves garlic, crushed
Bouquet garni: thyme, minced parsley, chervil
1 teaspoon fennel powder
Grated rind of 1 orange
1 large potato, peeled and diced fine
1 teaspoon turmeric
Salt and pepper
5 cups chicken broth

GARNISH

6 canapés of bread fried in butter
6 soft poached eggs

Sauté the onions and leek in the olive oil until they begin to color. Add all the ingredients except the garnish. Cover and simmer gently 20 minutes. (You can substitute water and 4 teaspoons of chicken soup concentrate for the broth.) Put a canapé of fried bread in each hot wide soup plate and top each with a soft poached egg. Carefully ladle the hot soup around the eggs. *Serves 6*

Garlic Soup with Poached Eggs #1

6 cloves garlic, crushed
1 fennel bulb, sliced fine
½ cup chopped onions
½ cup diced carrots
1 leek, sliced
2 cups water

Salt and pepper
5 cups chicken broth

GARNISH

6 canapés of bread fried in butter
6 soft poached eggs

Cook the garlic and all the vegetables in the water, salt, and pepper until tender, then purée with the cooking water. Add the chicken broth and simmer 2 minutes. Put a canapé in each warmed soup plate, top with a soft poached egg, and pour the hot soup over them. *Serves 6*

Garlic Soup with Poached Eggs #2

8 cloves garlic
4 tablespoons ham fat
2 tablespoons flour
4½ cups boiling chicken or beef
    consommé

2 tablespoons minced parsley
4 soft poached eggs

ACCOMPANIMENT

Croutons fried in butter

Crush 4 of the garlic cloves, and slice the other 4. Put all in a heavy pot with the ham fat over low heat and stir until the garlic colors ivory, but do not let burn. Stir in the flour and when smooth add the boiling consommé. Cover and simmer gently 15 minutes. Add the parsley. Put a soft poached egg in each warmed soup plate. Pour the soup over the eggs. Pass a bowl of croutons.

VARIATION: When the soup begins to simmer add ½ cup tomato purée and 1 or 2 teaspoons powdered fennel. *Serves 4*

Spanish Egg Soup

This is an unusual and delicious luncheon dish.

½ cup fresh breadcrumbs
2 cups light cream
2 cups milk
3 cloves garlic, crushed
3 tablespoons butter
3 tablespoons olive oil
⅓ cup sliced almonds, toasted

Salt and pepper
3 teaspoons cumin powder

GARNISH

4 or 5 slices buttered toast
Soft poached eggs

Soak the crumbs in the cream and milk for 10 minutes in a saucepan. Put the garlic, butter, and oil in a heavy pot and stir until the garlic colors ivory, then stir in the almonds. Boil up the cream mixture and pour it into the pot. Season with salt and pepper and stir in the cumin powder. Cook 5 minutes over low heat. Put a slice of crisp buttered toast in the bottom of each warmed wide soup plate, put 1 or 2 eggs, according to your preferences, on top of the toast, and add the hot soup. *Serves 4 to 5*

Lemon and Rice Soup

⅓ cup Patna rice or Indian rice
Grated rind of 1 lemon
⅓ cup lemon juice
2 teaspoons sugar
6 cups chicken broth

3 tablespoons minced parsley
Salt and pepper

ACCOMPANIMENT

Croutons fried in butter

Wash the rice and soak it all day with the lemon rind and juice, sugar, and broth. Rice, like dried legumes, cooks more quickly when soaked. Twenty minutes before serving, bring the broth to a simmer, cover tightly, and cook until the rice is tender. It should be done in 15 minutes. Add the parsley and check the seasoning. Serve with croutons. *Serves 6*

Cheese Soup with Veal Broth

8 cups veal broth
4 tablespoons flour
1½ cups shredded Gruyère cheese
Salt and pepper
Dash of cayenne

¼ teaspoon nutmeg
4 whole eggs

ACCOMPANIMENT

Bowl of croutons fried in butter

Blend a little broth with the flour until smooth, then mix in the rest of the broth. Cook uncovered in the top of a double boiler over simmering water for 15 minutes. Add the cheese and stir until it is melted and smooth. Add the seasonings. Beat the eggs in a warmed tureen until thick, then whisk in the hot soup. Serve a bowl of crisp croutons. *Serves 8*

Potage Gruyère *(Gruyère Cheese Soup)*

2 cups shredded French Gruyère
    cheese
3 tablespoons flour
4 tablespoons butter
1 cup white wine, Neuchâtel for
    instance
4 cups milk
4 eggs, thickly beaten

Chicken bouillon
Salt and freshly ground pepper
¼ teaspoon nutmeg
1 jigger Kirsch

ACCOMPANIMENT

Croutons fried in butter

Toss the cheese and flour together. Melt the butter in the top of a double boiler over simmering water and stir in the cheese mixture. Add the wine and stir until the cheese is melted and smooth. Scald the milk, stir it into the beaten eggs, then whisk this into the cheese mixture. When the mixture is smooth and hot and a little thickened, add enough hot chicken bouillon to thin until it is the consistency of heavy cream. Add the seasonings and the Kirsch. This recipe may remind you of fondue—well, it tastes like it. Pass a bowl of croutons and serve a chilled Neuchâtel if you wish. *Serves 6 to 8*

Dutch Beer Soup

2 tablespoons flour
2 tablespoons butter
5 cups Dutch beer
1 teaspoon light brown sugar
¼ teaspoon ginger
½ teaspoon cumin powder
¼ teaspoon nutmeg

¼ teaspoon cinnamon
1 tablespoon grated orange rind
Salt

GARNISH

4 slices bread fried in butter

Cook the flour in the butter until the mixture colors ivory. Blend in a little beer with a rubber spatula until smooth, then add the rest of the beer and all the seasonings. Simmer gently 15 minutes, stirring constantly. Put a slice of fried bread in each soup plate and divide the soup into the plates. Serves 4

Beer Cream Soup

4½ cups chicken broth
2 cups dark beer
1½ cups rye breadcrumbs
Salt and freshly ground pepper
¼ teaspoon nutmeg

¼ teaspoon cinnamon
⅓ cup heavy cream

GARNISH

Rye bread croutons fried in butter

Mix the broth, beer, and crumbs, cover, and simmer 15 minutes. Mash through a sieve. Add the seasonings and the cream. Reheat and serve in warmed soup plates and sprinkle the top of each plate of soup with croutons. Serves 6

Red Wine Soup

⅓ cup butter
3 tablespoons oil
2 small leeks, sliced fine
⅓ cup finely diced carrots
1 small white turnip, peeled and diced fine
⅓ cup finely chopped onion
1 teaspoon chervil
1 teaspoon basil

1¼ cups good red Burgundy, heated
1 tablespoon brown sugar
6 or 7 cups hot beef bouillon
1 tablespoon semolina (cream wheat)

GARNISH

Minced fresh parsley or chervil
Crisp croutons fried in butter

Melt the butter in a pot, add the oil and all the vegetables. (The vegetables must be chopped fine as the soup is not sieved.) Stir over low heat until the vegetables begin to soften. Add the herbs, heated wine, and sugar, and boil to reduce to half. Empty all into the top of a double boiler, add the hot bouillon, cover, and cook 45 minutes over simmering water, then add the semolina and cook 10 minutes more, uncovered. Stir several times. Sprinkle each serving with the fresh herb and pass a bowl of croutons. *Serves 6 to 8*

Armenian Yoghurt Soup

5 cups chicken broth	1/3 cup minute tapioca or vermicelli
½ cup chopped onions	¼ cup minced parsley
4 tablespoons butter	3 or 4 cups yoghurt
Salt and pepper	3 or 4 tablespoons minced fresh mint

Heat the broth to boiling. Sauté the onions in the butter until they soften, add the boiling broth, and simmer covered for 5 minutes then add the tapioca or vermicelli and the parsley. Cover and simmer 15 minutes. Whip the yoghurt, whisk it into the soup, and cook 5 minutes. Add the mint. Serve hot or cold. *Serves 8 in soup cups*

Russian and Spanish Soups, Borschts, Gazpachos, Etc.

Preparing Beets for Soup

To preserve the color and flavor of beets, cook them separately. Scrub the beets clean, as the water they cook in usually goes into the soup. Cut the stems not less than an inch from the beets to prevent their "bleeding"—they should be deep red after they have cooked. Cook the beets in 2 or 3 cups of water, or water as specified in the recipes. Young, small beets take 18 to 20 minutes to cook; old, large beets take longer. Test with a cake tester. When the beets are done, skin them and slice or dice as specified. Sometimes they are puréed.

Borscht

2 bunches new beets	1 tablespoon brown sugar
2 cups water	½ teaspoon caraway seeds or
2 cups beef consommé	caraway powder
1½ cups tomato purée	¼ teaspoon powdered clove
½ cup red wine	
Salt and pepper	GARNISH
1 onion, chopped	Sour cream
Grated rind and juice of 1 orange	

Prepare the beets as directed and cook them in the water until just tender. Drain them and put the beet water in the beef consommé. Skin the beets and add them to the liquid with all the other ingredients. Cover and simmer gently 30 minutes. Remove 2 beets, dice them, and reserve. Strain the soup through a sieve, or, better, purée it in a blender. Return the diced beets to the strained soup or purée and check the seasoning. It may need more spices, salt, pepper, and sugar. Some like a little lemon juice or vinegar with beet soup. This soup is good cold in summer or hot in winter. Pass a bowl of sour cream to add to the soup. *Serves 8*

Baltic Borscht

2 pounds breast or neck of lamb; or
   1 2½-pound chicken; or 2 pounds
   smooth, fat tripe (not honeycomb
   tripe)
Half a good-sized cabbage, shredded
4 potatoes, peeled and diced
1 carrot, sliced
1 parsley root, scraped and diced
½ cup sliced celery
½ cup chopped onions
⅓ cup Patna rice
Salt and pepper

1 bunch new beets
2½ cups water
2 tablespoons vinegar
2 tablespoons tomato paste
2 tablespoons sugar
Salt and pepper
2 tablespoons minced chives
2 tablespoons minced parsley

GARNISH

Bowl of sour cream

The lamb is cooked in 2 quarts of water 1½ hours, then the vegetables and rice are added, with salt and pepper, and cooked, covered, 30 minutes more. The chicken is cooked in 2 quarts water, covered, 30 minutes at a slow simmer, then the vegetables, rice, and salt and pepper are added and it is cooked 30 minutes more. The tripe is prepared by blanching in boiling water and draining: this is done three times. Then it is put in a kettle with 1½ cups minced vegetables (onions, carrots, and white turnips), 2 crushed cloves garlic, and 6 cups of water, covered and simmered 6 hours, then drained, rinsed, and cut in 2-inch squares. It is then cooked with the same vegetables as the lamb or chicken, the rice, and 2 quarts of water, covered, for 30 minutes. Whether the soup is made with lamb, chicken, or tripe, add ½ teaspoon meat glaze and 3 teaspoons chicken soup concentrate for increased flavor. Scrub the beets and cut the stems a generous inch from the beet, then boil them until tender in 2½ cups of water and the vinegar. Skin them, cut them in julienne sticks, and return them to their cooking water. Add the tomato paste, sugar, salt and pepper. If lamb or chicken has been used, drain the meat out of the soup and serve separately. The tripe, of course, is left in the soup. Add the beet mixture to the soup with the chives and parsley. Reheat to serve and pass a bowl of sour cream. *Serves 8*

Borscht Froid (Cold Borscht)

Auberge du Lion d'Or, Cologny, Geneva

M. Jacques Lacombe says this is très agréable l'été. I say with enthusiasm—in spring and fall as well.

1¼ pounds new beets
¼ cup wine vinegar
2 medium-sized cucumbers, peeled
   and diced
1 white onion, diced
6 cups sour cream
3½ ounces fresh breadcrumbs
2 tablespoons sugar

Salt
1½ tablespoons English mustard

GARNISH

Bowl of diced cucumbers
Bowl of diced beets
Bowl of 3 chopped hard-cooked eggs

Scrub the beets and cut the stems a generous inch from the beet. Boil them until tender with 1 tablespoon of the vinegar to the water. Skin and dice them, reserving ⅔ cup of garnish. Put the rest in an earthenware bowl with the rest of the vinegar. Peel and dice the cucumbers, reserve ½ cup for garnish, and add the rest to the beets. Add the diced onion, sour cream, breadcrumbs, sugar, salt, and mustard to the beet mixture. Let the mixture marinate 12 hours, then purée it in a blender. Serve cold, with garnishes in bowls. Serves 8 to 10

Polish Borscht

BROTH

1½ pound chuck
1 thick slice ham
Game bird or duck carcass, if
   available
1 cup chopped onions
2 carrots, chopped
2 leeks, sliced
1 teaspoon marjoram
Salt and pepper
Water to cover

THE BORSCHT

½ cup dried mushrooms
2 smoked pork chops
1 cup water
2 bunches beets
2½ cups water
1 tablespoon sugar
Juice of 1 lemon

GARNISH

Bowl of sour cream

Put all the ingredients for the broth in a large kettle, bring to the simmer, skim, cover, and cook gently 2 hours. Meanwhile rinse the mushrooms in boiling water and soak them 1 hour in 1 cup of water. When the broth has cooked, add the pork chops and the mushrooms with their soaking water. Simmer 30 minutes. Remove and discard any bones, remove all the meats, cut them in cubes and return the cubes to the soup.

Meanwhile scrub the beets and cut the stems a generous inch from the beet. Cook them in the 2½ cups water, with the sugar and lemon juice, until tender. Skin the beets, cut in julienne sticks, and add them and their cooking water to the soup. Check the seasonings: more lemon juice, salt, and sugar may be needed. Pass the sour cream. *Serves 8*

Russian Borscht

2 bunches new beets	Salt and pepper
3 cups water	2 tablespoons vinegar
½ cup tomato purée	2 tablespoons brown sugar
1 small young cabbage	2 bay leaves
½ cup diced carrots	
1 cup diced onions	GARNISH
2 cups cubed potatoes (optional)	Bowl of sour cream
4 cups beef bouillon	

Scrub the beets and cut the stem a generous inch above the beet. Cook them in the water until tender, then skin and dice them. Return them to their cooking water and add the tomato purée. Quarter the cabbage and slice in the thinnest possible slices. Put the cabbage in another kettle with the other vegetables, the bouillon, and all the seasonings and cook, covered, for 20 minutes. Add the beets and their water and check the seasonings; the soup may need more vinegar and sugar. Pass the sour cream. *Serves 10*

Ukranian Borscht

1½ pounds beets	1 ready-to-eat German or Polish
4 cups water	sausage
2 tablespoons brown sugar	3 tablespoons butter
2 tablespoons vinegar	2 cups boiling beef stock
4 ounces salt pork, sliced and diced	Salt and pepper
2 potatoes, peeled and diced	
½ cup chopped onions	GARNISH
2 cloves garlic, crushed	Bowl of sour cream

Scrub the beets and cut the stems a generous inch above the beet. Boil them until tender in the water. Skin and slice them, purée them with their cooking water, and add the sugar and vinegar. Sauté the diced salt pork until it begins to color, then add the potatoes and onions. Cover and steam tender over very low heat, shaking often to prevent burning.

Add the garlic, salt, and pepper and put all into the beet purée. Slice the sausage and sauté in the butter on both sides until golden; add it to the purée and add the beef stock. Check the seasonings. The soup should be quite thick, but if it is too thick, add a little boiling water or stock. Reheat to serve and pass the sour cream. *Serves 8*

Gazpacho Extremeño *(Estremaduran Gazpacho)*
Hotel Ritz, Madrid

M. Georges Force is the French *Inspector de Cocina* of this "most beautiful hotel in the world." In fine weather, tables are set out on the terrace and garden below, overlooking the Prado, which makes dining here the most attractive in Madrid. The fine food reflects the varied career of M. Force. He has been chef at the Barclay in Philadelphia and also in Sweden, Malta, and Bombay.

3 cloves garlic, crushed	1 teaspoon red pepper
½ green pepper, chopped fine	2 teaspoons cumin powder
1 large tomato, skinned and sliced	1 quart water
½ cup olive oil	
1 cucumber, peeled and chopped fine	GARNISHES
1 medium-sized onion, chopped fine	Croutons fried in oil
6 slices French bread, cubed	Cubed cucumbers
¼ cup wine vinegar	Cubed green pepper
Salt	Skinned, chopped tomatoes
	Sliced green onions

Put the crushed garlic in a blender with the chopped green pepper and the sliced tomato. Purée until smooth, then add the olive oil. Purée until liquid. Put all the rest of the ingredients and seasonings in the water and let stand 30 minutes. Add the puréed liquid and purée the mixture in the blender, a little at a time, until it is very smooth. Chill several hours. Stir well before putting the soup in wide soup plates. Serve the garnishes in bowls for spooning into the soup. *Serves 8 to 10*

Rassolnik *(Russian Veal-Kidney Soup)*

½ cup Patna rice
1½ cups chicken broth
2 veal kidneys
4 tablespoons butter
6 or 7 cups veal or chicken broth
1 carrot, chopped fine

1 onion, chopped fine
2 pickled cucumbers, sliced

GARNISH

Sliced fresh cucumbers
Sliced hard-cooked eggs

Soak the rice several hours in the 1½ cups chicken broth. Sauté the kidneys quickly in butter so they are golden on both sides. Cut them in half laterally and cut the segments apart. Put them in the veal or chicken broth with the carrot, onion, and cucumbers. (The Russians pickle cucumbers in salt brine for 3 or more weeks. Dill pickles may be used instead.) Cover and simmer gently 15 minutes. Strain out the kidneys and set aside. Put the rice and its broth into the soup, cover, and simmer slowly 18 minutes or until the rice is done. Return the kidneys to the soup. Reheat to serve. Garnish each soup plate with sliced fresh cucumbers and slices of egg. Pearl barley may be used instead of rice; it is soaked and cooked the same way. *Serves 6 to 8*

Cold Cucumber and Beet Soup

4 ounces pickled cucumber,
    coarsely chopped
1 cup buttermilk
1 bunch new beets
3 cups water
1 teaspoon powdered fennel
Salt and pepper

GARNISH

½ pound fresh shrimp
3 hard-cooked eggs, sliced
¼ cup chopped chives
1 fresh cucumber, sliced

Marinate the chopped cucumber in the buttermilk 1 hour in the refrigerator. Scrub the beets and cut the stem a generous inch above the beet and cook them in the water until tender. Drain the beets, reserving the cooking water. Skin the beets and cut them in julienne sticks. Return them to the cooking water and add the fennel, salt, and pepper. When the beets are cool, stir in the cucumber mixture and chill the soup. Cook the shrimp 1½ minutes, shell them, cut them in half lengthwise, and chill them. Serve the cold soup in wide soup plates, dividing the garnishes among the plates. *Serves 4*

Stchi *(Russian Beef and Cabbage Soup)*

3 pounds chuck or brisket of beef
2 quarts water
2 onions, sliced
2 carrots, sliced
2 white turnips, peeled and sliced
3 tablespoons chopped parsley
Salt and pepper

1 new cabbage, shredded
4 ounces spinach, chopped
4 ounces sorrel, chopped

GARNISH

Bowl of sour cream

Put the meat in a large soup kettle and add the water, bring to a simmer, and skim. Add the onions, carrots, turnips, and parsley, cover, and cook slowly 2½ hours. After 1 hour add salt and pepper and the cabbage and after 15 minutes more add the spinach and sorrel. (If sorrel is not available use chopped watercress and 2 or 3 tablespoons of lemon juice.) If the soup is too thick, add a little boiling water. Serve the meat separately. Pass the sour cream to spoon into the hot soup. *Serves 6 to 8*

Gazpacho Andaluz *(Andalusian Gazpacho)*
Ritz Hotel, Barcelona

Senor Gotanegra is chef at this charming hotel. His gazpacho is unusual and delicious. The addition of mayonnaise makes it smooth as silk.

8 ripe tomatoes, skinned
3 green peppers
1 medium-sized onion
1 clove garlic, crushed
2 cucumbers, peeled
1 teaspoon red pepper
Salt and freshly ground pepper
1 cup water

2 tablespoons wine vinegar
1 cup oil mayonnaise (see index)

GARNISHES

Diced cucumbers
Skinned, seeded, chopped tomatoes
Finely sliced green onions
Small croutons fried in butter

Chop all the vegetables and purée with the seasonings, water, and vinegar until mixture is very smooth. Check the seasoning, then whisk in the mayonnaise. Chill until ready to serve. Serve the garnishes in separate bowls so that each person can spoon a little of each into his soup. *Serves 6 to 8*

Gazpacho Blanc *(White Gazpacho)*

2 ripe tomatoes, skinned	3 tablespoons breadcrumbs
1 sweet green pepper	1 cup mild vinegar
1 hot pepper	Salt and freshly ground pepper
1 cucumber, peeled	2 cups water
6 cloves garlic, crushed	2 cups heavy cream
3 cups chicken or veal broth	2 tablespoons chopped parsley

Grind all the vegetables and the garlic as fine as possible. Add all the other ingredients except the cream and parsley. Let the mixture infuse for several hours. Slowly stir in the cream. Sprinkle with parsley. Chill and serve very cold from a tureen. *Serves 8*

Vegetable Soups

Asparagus Soup

1 bunch asparagus (2½ pounds)	⅛ teaspoon nutmeg
2 cups water	2 egg yolks
Salt	
½ cup chopped onion	ACCOMPANIMENT
3½ cups rich chicken stock	Buttered croutons
1 cup heavy cream	

Trim the coarsest skin off the lower part of the asparagus stalks. Cut off 3 inches of the tips and reserve. Cut the stalks in very thin slices for maximum flavor. Cook them in 2 cups salted water 30 minutes over low heat, tightly covered (10 minutes in a pressure cooker). Press the asparagus against a coarse sieve to extract as much pulp as possible. Cook the tips with the onion in the chicken stock, covered, 10 to 12 minutes, or until the tips ard tender. Remove and reserve half the tips and purée the rest with the sieved pulp and the stock. When ready to serve, season the cream with nutmeg, scald it, mix it with the egg yolks, and whisk into the hot soup. Return the whole tips to the soup before serving. Serve with crisp buttered croutons. *Serves 6 to 8*

Potage Elizabeth Jubilee *(Chicken Soup with Asparagus)*
John Bainbridge, Executive Chef, RMS *Queen Elizabeth II*

Mr. Bainbridge was most enthusiastic about contributing this elegant soup to mark the twenty-fifth year of the reign of Queen Elizabeth II.

6 large leeks	2 ounces white chicken meat, diced
4 tablespoons butter	1 ounce York ham, diced
3 or 4 tablespoons flour	1 ounce whole part of leeks, cut in
6 cups rich chicken stock, boiling	julienne sticks
1 cup light cream	2 tablespoons butter
Salt and pepper	12 cooked asparagus tips

Prepare a rich chicken stock with chicken parts and vegetables but use leeks instead of onions. When it is done, strain it. Dice the white part of 6 large leeks and cook slowly in butter without browning. Stir in the flour and when mixture is smooth, slowly add the boiling stock, stirring continuously. Simmer for 1 hour, gently, to prevent evaporation. Cool and pass through a fine sieve. Add the cream and season with salt and pepper. Before serving add the diced chicken and ham (if York ham is not available, use good cooked ham, diced fine). Cook the julienne white of leeks in 2 tablespoons butter and when tender add them and the cooked asparagus tips to the soup. Bring gently to a simmer and divide the soup into hot plates, being careful to have 2 asparagus tips in each plate. *Serves 6*

Artichoke Soup

4 large artichokes	6 ounces fresh button mushrooms
6 cups warm water	3 tablespoons butter
Juice of 1 lemon	¼ cup sliced green onions
1 quart rich chicken stock	1 cup heavy cream
1 clove garlic, crushed	2 large egg yolks
1 tablespoon cornstarch	3 tablespoons minced parsley
1 cup dry white wine	

Wash the artichokes and put them in a 4-quart pot. Add the 6 cups of warm water and the lemon juice, cover, and boil for 35 minutes. Drain the artichokes upside down. Take off all the leaves, and cut out and discard the choke. Firmly take the tip of each leaf and scrape all the meaty part into a bowl. Slice the hearts, add, and purée all in a blender with 1 cup of the chicken stock. Rinse out the blender with another cup of stock. Boil the rest of the stock with the garlic 1 minute and combine all. Blend the cornstarch with the wine, add, and heat until the mixture thickens a little. Clean the mushrooms, melt the butter in a pan, stir in the green onions, and add the mushrooms, and bake 5 minutes in 350° oven. When ready to serve, reheat the soup, scald the cream, mix it with the egg yolks, and whisk into the soup. Do not boil again. Add the baked mushrooms and the parsley. A great party soup. *Serves 6 to 8*

Cream of Jerusalem Artichokes

1 pound Jerusalem artichokes	4 cups hot chicken consommé
1½ cups boiling salted water	1 teaspoon chervil
3 leeks, sliced fine	1 cup heavy cream
3 shallots, minced	2 egg yolks
3 tablespoons butter	3 tablespoons chopped parsley

Remove any blemishes from the artichoke tubers and scrub them; their skin is too tender to peel. Slice them and cook in the boiling salted water until very tender. Mash them with the cooking water through a coarse sieve to remove any coarse skin. Soften the leeks and shallots in the butter in a saucepan until they begin to color. Add 2 cups of the hot consommé, cook 5 minutes and then add the purée and the rest of the consommé. Cover and simmer gently 2 or 3 minutes. Add the chervil. When ready to serve reheat the soup, scald the cream, mix it with the egg yolks, and whisk into the soup. Add the parsley. To extend this soup, cook 1½ cups of potatoes cut in small cubes with the artichoke tubers and mash them through the sieve. *Serves 6 to 8*

Avocado Soup

1 large ripe avocado or 2 small ones
4 cups chicken stock
1 tablespoon grated white onion
2 or 3 teaspoons curry powder
Salt and pepper
1 cup heavy cream
1/3 cup Madeira

GARNISHES
Avocado balls
Pitted Bing cherries
Melon balls
Seedless grapes

Skin the avocado, remove the seed, and sieve or purée the flesh with some of the stock. Add the rest of the stock, the onion, and the seasonings. Check for salt and pepper, and add the cream and wine. Serve hot or cold with any of the garnishes you choose. This makes a delightful cold summer soup. *Serves 6.*

Fresh Green-Bean Soup

3 slices bacon
3 tablespoons butter
½ cup diced onions
1 leek, sliced
1 clove garlic, crushed
½ cup diced carrots

Salt and pepper
Ham bone
7 or 8 cups water
1 pound green beans, cut in ½-inch
  lengths

Fry the bacon in the butter until crisp, remove, crumble, and reserve. Put the vegetables and the garlic in the fat and stir 2 minutes, then add the seasoning, ham bone, and water. Cover and cook slowly 1 hour, add the beans, and cook another 20 minutes. Purée half of the soup and add to the rest of the soup along with the bacon. *Serves 8*

VARIATION: Green-Bean and Tomato Soup. Use 2 cups of chopped tomatoes in purée and only 6 cups of water.

Hungarian Green-Bean Soup

1 pound green beans, cut in ½-inch
   lengths
½ cup chopped onions
½ cup thinly sliced celery
1 potato, peeled and diced
½ cup finely diced carrot
1 whole clove garlic
6 cups veal or chicken stock

Salt and pepper
2 tablespoons butter
2 tablespoons flour
2 teaspoons sugar
1 cup sour cream
1 or 2 tablespoons sweet Hungarian
   paprika

The vegetables must be diced fine, as the soup is neither sieved nor puréed. Put all the vegetables and the garlic in a kettle with the stock, cover, and cook slowly 25 minutes. Season with salt and pepper to taste. Melt the butter, blend in the flour until the mixture is smooth and let it color. Stir in a little soup, then add the mixture to the soup and simmer 1 minute. Add the sugar. Reheat the soup. Mix the sour cream with the paprika, warm it, and stir into the soup. *Serves 6 to 8*

Puréed Beet Soup

2 bunches fresh beets
7 cups water
Salt and freshly ground pepper
4 green onions, chopped
2 tablespoons butter
Salt and pepper
2 or 3 tablespoons tarragon vinegar
3 eggs, beaten
Chopped chives

POTATO PUREE

6 potatoes
Hot milk
2 tablespoons butter
Salt and pepper

Wash the beets and cut the stems more than 1 inch from the beets. The cooking water is used in the soup. Boil the beets in the water until tender. Drain the beets, reserving the cooking water; skin and slice them. Soften the onions a minute in the butter and purée them with the beets and the beet water. Add salt, pepper, and vinegar to taste. Boil the potatoes, purée with the hot milk until smooth, and add the butter and salt and pepper. They may be kept hot in a baking dish in the oven. When ready to serve, reheat the soup, whisk the beaten eggs into it, and add the chopped chives. The potatoes and soup are served at the same time—a French custom and a very good combination for lunch or supper. *Serves 6*

Broccoli Soup

1 bunch young broccoli
Cold salted water
1½ cups salted boiling water
⅓ cup finely diced onions
3 tablespoons butter
1 small can vegetable juice

2 cups chicken stock
1 cup cream
Salt and pepper

GARNISH

Bowl of grated Gruyère cheese

Young broccoli makes fine soup; the old is too strong. Soak the broccoli in cold salted water ½ hour. Drain and rinse it. Remove the hard outer skin from the stems, slice them fine and put them in the bottom of a pot. Separate the flowerets and put them on top. Pour 1½ cups salted boiling water over them, cover, and cook until broccoli is tender—12 or 15 minutes. (A pressure cooker takes only 1 cup water and less than 2 minutes to cook.) Remove ½ cup flowerets and reserve. Meanwhile soften the onion in the butter until it begins to color. Purée it with the rest of the broccoli and its cooking water. Add the vegetable juice and stock to the purée, thin with cream, and check for salt and pepper. Return the flowerets to the soup. Reheat to serve and pass the cheese.
Serves 8

Brussels Sprouts Soup

1 quart brussels sprouts
3 tablespoons butter
3 tablespoons minced onion
6 cups hot chicken or veal
  consommé

2 tablespoons cornstarch
2 tablespoons lemon juice
¼ teaspoon nutmeg
3 tablespoons chopped parsley

Trim and wash the sprouts. Remove some of the outer leaves from 16 sprouts to make them small for garnishing and set these aside. Stir the removed leaves and the rest of the sprouts in the butter with the onion 1 or 2 minutes in a large pot, then add 5 cups of the hot consommé, cover, and cook until the sprouts are tender. Purée the contents of the pot. Cook the small sprouts in the remaining cup consommé until they are tender, then add them and the liquid to the purée. Reheat the soup; blend the cornstarch with the lemon juice, and add to thicken the soup until the consistency is like cream. Add the nutmeg and parsley to the top.

VARIATION: Cream of Brussels Sprouts. Omit the cornstarch. When the soup is hot, scald ¾ cup of heavy cream, mix it with 2 egg yolks, and whisk into the soup. *Serves 8*

Cream of Fava Bean *(Creamed Broad Bean Soup)*

1½ pounds fava beans (broad beans)
4 strips bacon
2 tablespoons butter
1 cup diced onions
½ cup diced peeled white turnips
½ cup diced carrots
½ cup sliced celery
Salt and pepper

4 cups water
3 teaspoons chicken soup
    concentrate
Light cream

ACCOMPANIMENT

Grated cheese or buttered croutons

Shell the beans and wash them. Sauté the bacon in the butter until it is crisp. Remove the bacon, crumble it, and set it aside. Sauté the onion in the fat until it begins to soften, then stir in the beans and the other vegetables. Stir the mixture a minute and season with salt and pepper. Mix the water and the soup concentrate, bring to a boil, and pour over the vegetables. Cover and simmer gently until the beans are tender, about 20 minutes. Remove ½ cup of beans and purée the contents of the pot. Thin the soup with light cream to a creamy consistency. Put the bacon crumbles and the reserved whole beans in the soup, and pass cheese or croutons if you wish. *Serves 8 or more*

Cream of Chard

1½ pounds chard
2 cups chicken or veal stock
Salt and pepper
1 onion, chopped
2 tablespoons butter or bacon fat
1 cup light cream
Milk or stock for thinning

ACCOMPANIMENT

Grated cheese, or croutons fried in
    butter

Chard makes a very good soup. Wash and trim it. Cut the stalks in 1-inch lengths and simmer them 2 minutes in 1 cup of the stock, covered. Add salt and pepper. Shred the chard leaves, add them to the pot with a little more stock, cover tightly and cook slowly until chard is tender. (It takes 1½ minutes in the pressure cooker). Soften the onion in the butter or bacon fat and stir into the chard. Purée with the rest of the stock. Add the cream. Thin the soup with milk or stock to the consistency of cream. Reheat and serve in cups with either garnish. *Serves 6 or more*

Cabbage and Tomato Soup

1 medium-sized white or red
  cabbage
4 tablespoons butter
1 cup chopped onions
Salt and pepper
4 cups vegetable juice

1 can carrot juice
1 cup tomato purée
2 teaspoons powdered fennel

GARNISH

Bowl of sour cream

This is a fine quick soup for a large family. Shred the cabbage quite fine. Blanch it with boiling water and drain it. Melt the butter in a soup kettle and soften the onions in it until they begin to color. Stir in the cabbage and add salt and pepper. Heat the juices and the tomato purée with the fennel in a separate pot. Pour over the cabbage; if the liquid doesn't quite cover add a little boiling water. Cover and cook slowly until the cabbage is tender. New cabbage will be done in 18 or 20 minutes. Remove 1 cup of the cabbage and set aside. Purée the rest of the soup. Add the reserved cabbage. Serve the soup in cups. Pass the sour cream. A cup of grapefruit juice may be added if the carrot juice makes the soup too sweet for your taste. Bottled grapefruit juice (not canned) is used to flavor soups. A little of it can do a lot. *Serves 8 or more*

Cabbage Soup with Red Wine *(Limousin)*

4 ounces salt pork, diced fine
1 small new cabbage, shredded fine
Salt and pepper
5 cups hot beef bouillon
1 cup dry red wine

ACCOMPANIMENT

Bowl of crisp croutons fried in butter

Fry the pork in a soup kettle until golden and crisp. Scoop out the pieces and reserve them. Soften the cabbage in the pork fat, stirring continuously so that it doesn't brown. Season with salt and pepper and add the hot bouillon. Cover and simmer 15 minutes. Drain out 1½ cups of cabbage and purée it, then return it to the soup. This gives body to the soup. Return the pork pieces to the soup. Heat the wine, put it in the bottom of a tureen, and pour the hot soup over it. Pass the croutons. *Serves 6*

Cabbage in Consommé

1 small new cabbage, quartered
3 tablespoons butter
⅓ cup water
Salt and pepper
½ to 1 teaspoon powdered caraway

6 or 7 cups beef or chicken stock

ACCOMPANIMENT

Cheese sticks (see index)

Soak the cabbage in cold water until it is crisp. Drain it and put it in a heavy soup pot with the butter and ⅓ cup water. Cover and steam tender—about 15 minutes. (A pressure cooker takes 2 minutes.) Cut up the cabbage, season it with a little salt and pepper and the caraway, and purée with 1 or 2 cups of the consommé. Add the rest of the consommé and reheat to serve. Cheese sticks are good with this. *Serves 8*

Cream of Cabbage Soup #1

6 slices bacon, diced
3 tablespoons butter
½ cup chopped onions
1 small young cabbage, shredded
6 cups boiling water
Salt and pepper

1 cup light cream
⅓ cup grated Gruyère or Parmesan
   cheese

ACCOMPANIMENT

Buttered croutons

Sauté the bacon in the butter in the bottom of the soup kettle and when the bacon is partly crisp, stir in the onions, cook until they soften, and then stir in the cabbage. Cook 2 minutes, and add 6 cups of boiling water. Add salt and pepper, cover, and cook 20 minutes. Remove 2 cups of cabbage, purée the rest of the soup, and return the cabbage to it. Mix the cream and the cheese and cook over low heat until the cheese is melted. Add to the soup. Serve hot with buttered croutons. *Serves 6 to 8*

Cream of Cabbage Soup #2

3 cups finely shredded cabbage
1 bunch green onions, minced
3 tablespoons butter
1 small potato, finely diced
½ cup water
Salt and freshly ground pepper
4 cups hot chicken broth

1 cup cream
1 teaspoon curry powder, or more

ACCOMPANIMENT

Bowl of grated Gruyère or Parmesan
   cheese

Put the shredded cabbage in a wooden chopping bowl and chop fine. The soup does not have to be puréed unless you choose. Cook the onions in the butter in a heavy pot a few seconds, then stir in the potato. Add the cabbage, water, salt, and pepper. Cover and steam over low heat until the cabbage is tender—about 15 minutes. Be sure it does not burn. Add the hot broth. Mix the cream with the curry powder (use more curry powder if you like) and add. Simmer a minute, then serve in hot soup plates. Pass the cheese. *Serves 6*

Cabbage and Potato Soup with Knackwurst

4 ounces salt pork, diced
3 tablespoons butter
½ cup diced onions
3 medium-sized potatoes, diced
½ new cabbage, shredded
Salt and pepper
6 cups chicken broth, or 6 cups
    water and 3 teaspoons chicken
    soup concentrate

3 or 4 knackwurst
Dijon mustard
Oil
1 cup sour cream

Fry the salt pork in the butter until crisp, then scoop out the pork pieces and reserve them. Stir the onions in the fat and when they color add the potatoes and cook them 2 minutes. Add the cabbage, salt and pepper, and the broth or water and soup concentrate. Cover and cook slowly 20 minutes or until the cabbage is tender. Add the knackwurst and cook 10 minutes. Take out the knackwurst, skin it, and cut it in slices. Spread each slice with mustard and just before serving brown them in a little oil. Reheat the soup, add the reserved pork pieces, and stir in the sour cream. Put 2 slices of knackwurst on top of each plate of soup. *Serves 6 to 8*

Savoy Cabbage Soup with Pork Sausage

¾ pound streaky salt pork
1 cup diced carrots
1 cup diced onions
2 bay leaves
2 quarts boiling water
2 cloves garlic, crushed
1 medium-sized curly cabbage,
    shredded
4 potatoes, quartered

1 large sausage (cervelas or
    Kolbasz), or 4 knackwurst

ACCOMPANIMENTS

Dijon mustard
Pickles
Black bread
Alsatian wine or beer

Blanch the pork in boiling water, drain, and rinse. Put it in a soup kettle with the carrots, onions, bay leaves, water, and garlic. Cover and cook slowly 1¾ hours or until the pork is tender. Add the cabbage and potatoes and the large sausage and cook 20 minutes or until the cabbage is tender. If knackwurst is used, add it 10 minutes later and cook it 10 minutes. (Overcooking sausage destroys its pungent flavor.) If more water is needed, add a little boiling water mixed with 2 teaspoons chicken soup concentrate. Drain out the pork and sausage and serve them with the accompaniments. Serve the soup in plates at the same time or serve as a first course as you choose. *Serves 6*

Carrot Soup

6 to 8 new carrots, sliced thin
½ cup chopped onions
3 tablespoons butter
1 12-ounce can vegetable juice
1 can carrot juice
1½ cans grapefruit juice (optional)

Salt and pepper
Lemon juice (optional)

GARNISH
Avocado balls or melon balls

Put the carrots and onions in a heavy pot with the butter and stir over low heat 1 to 2 minutes. Add 1 cup of the vegetable juice, cover, and cook until the carrots are tender. (This takes 2 minutes in a pressure cooker. Quick cooking for young vegetables retains all their fresh flavor.) Purée the contents of the pot in a blender and combine with the rest of the juices and salt and pepper. If you like, add lemon juice to taste. This delicious and refreshing soup may be served hot or cold. In summer it is nice garnished with fruit. *Serves 8*

Carrot and Tomato Soup

2 bunches new carrots
¾ cup diced onions
¼ cup butter
2 cups orange juice or grapefruit
    juice
Salt and pepper

2 cups tomato purée

GARNISH
Sour cream, or buttered croutons, or
    chopped parsley

Scrub the carrots and slice them thin. Cook the onions a minute in the butter then add the carrots and cook over low heat 2 or 3 minutes, covered. See that they do not burn. Add 1 cup of the juice and cook until the carrots are tender. (The pressure cooker takes 1½ minutes.) Purée the contents of the pot, rinsing out the blender with some of the juice. If you like the soup less sweet, use grapefruit juice. Add the tomato purée. Reheat to serve. This may also be served cold in summer. Garnish with sour cream or buttered croutons or just chopped parsley. *Serves 6*

Potage Crécy *(French Carrot Soup)*

1 bunch new carrots	1 tablespoon rice starch or
⅓ cup diced onions	cornstarch
¼ cup butter	Salt and pepper
½ cup hot water	
2 teaspoons minced fresh chervil	ACCOMPANIMENT
5 cups chicken stock	Croutons fried in butter

Scrub the carrots, slice them very thin, and stir them with the onions in the butter over low heat 2 minutes. Add ½ cup hot water, cover, and cook slowly until carrots are tender. Purée with the herb and some of the chicken stock, then add the rest of the stock. If the soup is too thin, blend a little with the rice starch or cornstarch and add. Season with salt and pepper. Reheat to serve. Pass the croutons.

VARIATION: When the soup is reheated, scald ¾ cup of heavy cream, mix it with 2 egg yolks, and whisk into the soup. Do not boil again. *Serves 6 to 8*

Cauliflower and Almond Soup

⅓ cup chopped onions	1 cup light cream, or more
3 tablespoons butter	
1 small cauliflower	GARNISH
Salt and pepper	½ cup sliced browned almonds
1 cup boiling water	
2 cups chicken broth	

Put the onions in a heavy pot with the butter and cook over low heat until the onions begin to color. Always choose white, young cauli-flower; the old is too strong for soup. Discard the coarsest stalks and leaves. Slice the tender leaves and the core very thin and add them to the onions. Slice the rest of the cauliflower and put it on top of the onion mixture, season with salt and pepper, and add 1 cup of boiling water. Cover tightly and simmer gently until the cauliflower is steamed tender. Purée the contents of the pot with the broth and thin with light cream to a creamy consistency. Reheat to serve. Sprinkle almonds over the top of each plate of soup. (Or pass a bowl of grated Gruyère or Parmesan cheese instead.)

VARIATION: Remove 6 or 8 small flowerets before puréeing and add one to each soup plate. *Serves 6 to 8*

Cauliflower and Watercress Soup

1 medium-sized white cauliflower
1 bunch watercress, stemmed and
   chopped
2 leeks, thinly sliced
1/3 cup butter
2 tablespoons lemon juice
3 cups salted boiling water

3 teaspoons chicken soup
   concentrate
1 cup heavy cream
2 egg yolks

ACCOMPANIMENT

Buttered croutons

Choose only a pure-white young cauliflower. Discard the coarsest leaves and stems. Slice the tender leaves and core very thin. Slice the flowerets. Chop the watercress very fine in a wooden bowl. Reserve 3 big tablespoons of it. Put the rest in a pot with the leeks, butter, and lemon juice. Soften 2 minutes over low heat then add all the cauliflower. Mix the boiling water and soup concentrate and pour it over the vegetables, cover, and cook 10 minutes or until the cauliflower is tender. Purée the contents of the pot. If the purée is too thick, add a little milk or water. Add the reserved watercress. Reheat to serve; scald the cream, mix with the egg yolks, and add. Do not boil again. Serve with a bowl of tiny buttered croutons. *Serves 6 to 8*

Celeriac Soup

2 celery roots (celeriac), peeled and
   diced
1/3 cup diced onions
1 cup diced potatoes
4 tablespoons butter
Salt and pepper
1/4 teaspoon nutmeg

4 to 5 cups chicken stock
1/2 cup heavy cream
1 egg yolk

GARNISH

Italian soup balls (see index), or
   buttered croutons

Peel the celery roots, slice, and then dice fine. Put in a heavy pot with the onions, potatoes, and the butter and stir a minute over low heat. Add the seasonings and 2 cups of the stock. Cover and cook until the vegetables are tender. Purée the contents of the pot with some more of the stock, then add the remaining stock. Reheat when ready to serve. Scald the cream, mix it with the egg yolk, and whisk into the soup.

VARIATION: Use beef stock instead of chicken stock. Omit the cream. When the soup is reheated, beat 2 eggs, put them in the bottom of a warm tureen, and whisk the hot soup into them. *Serves 6 to 8*

Cream of Celery

3 cups sliced celery and leaves
1 celery root, peeled and diced
1/3 cup chopped onions
3 tablespoons butter
1 large potato, diced
Salt and pepper
1½ cups boiling water

3 to 4 cups chicken stock
1 cup cream
2 egg yolks
1/3 cup chopped chives

GARNISH

Grated cheese or croutons

Prepare the celery and celery root. Soften the onions a little in the butter in a soup kettle, then add the celery, celery root, and potato. Add salt and pepper and the boiling water. Cover and cook over low heat until the vegetables are tender. Purée the contents of the pot with the cooking liquid, adding some stock if necessary; combine with the rest of the stock. If the soup is too thick, add a little stock or boiling water. Reheat before serving. Scald the cream, mix it with the egg yolks, and whisk into the hot soup. Do not boil again. Pass a bowl of either garnish. *Serves 6 to 8*

Celery Soup alla Rocca
Hotel della Rocca, Bazzano

This unusual and delicious soup is an old family recipe from the hotel which has been in the Rocchi family since 1796. Their guest book, or "book of documents," with letters and signatures from over 100 years looks like an Almanach de Gotha. Vittorio Rocchi and his wife are hosts of this charming inn. The dining garden, three terraces above the inn, has a backdrop of cypress trees. It's an enchanting sight when lights are played on the trees at night.

8 large stalks celery
3 inches of lemon peel
2 cups water
½ teaspoon salt
2 tablespoons olive oil
3 tablespoons minced parsley
2 cloves garlic, crushed
½ cup tomato purée

6 to 7 cups chicken or beef stock
6 Italian sausages

ACCOMPANIMENTS

Croutons fried in butter
Bowl of grated Gruyère or Parmesan
    cheese

This soup is one that used to be put on the back of the stove to ripen all day. It is a way to use the big outer stalks of a large bunch of Pascal celery. Cut the stalks in 1-inch lengths and put them in a heavy pot with the lemon peel, water, and salt. Cover and simmer gently 1 hour.

Meanwhile heat the olive oil, sauté the parsley and garlic a moment, add the tomato purée, cover, and simmer 10 minutes. When the celery is cooked, add the tomato mixture and the stock. Let the soup stand all day or overnight. An hour before serving, quickly brown the sausages, cut each in 4 pieces, put them into the soup, and simmer it 1 hour, covered. Serve in soup plates, with some celery and 3 or 4 pieces of sausage in each. Pass bowls of buttered croutons and cheese. *Serves 6 to 8*

Bazzano is an old Roman town. The surrounding countryside is dotted with castle ruins. One is the meeting place of the Compagnia dell'Arte dei Brentatori, a wine society founded in 1250. Vittorio Rocchi is the head of the society. Its dinner meetings celebrate the fine food and wine of Emilia, which means mainly Bologna. Their magnificent banquets are usually given to receive a new honorary member.

Celery and Tomato Soup

1 large bunch celery
3 large onions, sliced
2 carrots, diced
Roast and steak bones (lamb, beef,
     pork, etc.)
1 teaspoon beef extract
Salt and pepper
3 whole cloves
1 teaspoon thyme
1 teaspoon basil
1 teaspoon chervil

Juice of ½ lemon
1 cup dry white wine
1 tablespoon brown sugar
1 can vegetable juice
Water to just cover
1 15-ounce can tomato purée

GARNISH

Chopped parsley
Sour cream or croutons

Clean the celery and use all, including the leaves. Break the stalks in half and strip off the strings—this makes celery easier to purée. Put all the ingredients except the tomato purée in a big soup kettle, with just enough water to show when the vegetables are pressed down with a spoon. Cover and simmer 1¼ hours. Discard the bones and purée the soup. After it is puréed, it may have to be sieved to remove celery fibers. Add the tomato purée, and salt if needed. Add the parsley, and pass the sour cream or croutons. *Makes more than 2 quarts*

Turkey Celery Soup

Celery is good in any vegetable soup but in turkey soup it has always been a main ingredient.

Turkey carcass	1 teaspoon marjoram
Leftover gravy	1 teaspoon chervil
Leftover dressing	1 small can vegetable juice
1 cup chopped onions	Salt and pepper
1 cup chopped carrots	1 white turnip, peeled and diced
1 cup dry white wine	1 parsnip, diced
1 bunch celery, thinly sliced	Water to cover
1 teaspoon thyme	

Disjoint the carcass, break up as much as possible, and put it in the bottom of a large soup kettle. Add all the other ingredients. Cover and simmer gently 2 hours. Strain the soup and let it cool. This is a rich gamy soup, fine served as is or used as a base for other soups, especially mushroom or onion. Crisp buttered croutons may be served with it. Chill in the refrigerator, then store in screw-top jars. *Makes over 2 quarts*

Chestnut and Chicken Soup

STOCK

1 chicken breast
2 chicken thighs
1 carrot, sliced
1 onion, sliced
2 sprigs parsley
1 teaspoon basil
1 teaspoon tarragon
1 cup dry white wine
6 cups chicken stock

THE SOUP

1 pound fresh chestnuts
1 jigger cognac
Salt and pepper
1 cup heavy cream
2 egg yolks

GARNISH

½ cup browned sliced almonds

Put all the ingredients up to and including the chicken stock in a soup kettle, cover, and simmer 25 to 30 minutes. Make a slit in the flat side of each chestnut. Put them in cold water and bring to a boil and cook 1½ minutes. Drain 3 or 4 at a time out of the water and shell and skin them while they are warm. Cook in a little water or broth 12 to 15 minutes or until they are tender. Strain the soup. Take the chicken meat off the bones. Cut the breast in julienne sticks (makes about 1½ cups). Cut 1 cup of chicken meat in small pieces and purée it with the chestnuts in 2 cups of the broth in a blender. Rinse out the blender with another cup of broth. Combine with the rest of the soup. Blaze the julienne chicken in the cognac and add it to the soup, which should be creamy and smooth. Season with salt and pepper if needed. Reheat to serve. Scald the cream, mix with the egg yolks, and whisk into the soup. Do not boil again. Sprinkle a few almonds on top of each plate of soup. *Serves 8*

Chestnut and Game Soup

1 pound fresh chestnuts	**1 cup heavy cream**
½ cup Madeira	**2 egg yolks**
8 cups game soup (see index)	

Make a slit in the flat side of each chestnut. Put them in cold water and bring to a boil and cook 1½ minutes. Drain 3 or 4 at a time out of the water and shell and skin them while they are warm. Put them in 2 cups of the stock and cook, covered, 15 to 20 minutes. They may be tested with a cake straw. Reserve 2 chestnuts for each serving and marinate these in ½ cup Madeira an hour before serving. Purée the rest of the chestnuts with the liquid they cooked in, and adding stock if necessary. Combine the purée with the rest of the stock. Heat to serve. Scald the cream, add it to the egg yolks and whisk into the hot soup. Add the Madeira marinade to the soup. Put 2 chestnuts in each soup plate and add the soup. *Serves 6 to 8*

Potage aux Ciboulettes *(Chive Soup)*

½ cup finely chopped chives, closely packed	**6 cups boiling rich chicken broth**
⅓ cup chopped parsley	GARNISH
¼ cup finely chopped shallots	**Slice of buttered toasted French bread for each serving**
¼ cup finely chopped green onions	**Sour cream or grated cheese**
4 tablespoons butter	
2 tablespoons flour	

Prepare the vegetables and herbs, stir them in the butter a minute, then add the flour and when it is well blended add the boiling broth. Cover and simmer gently 10 minutes. Put either garnish in wide soup plates. If sour cream is used, put a big blob of it on each piece of toast, put one piece in each plate, and pour the soup around it. If cheese is used, put a thick layer of cheese on each piece of toast and put the pieces in a hot oven to melt and brown the cheese. Put a piece in each soup plate and add the soup. A soft poached egg may also be put on each piece of toast; the soft egg mixing with the soup is good. *Serves 5 to 6*

Collard Soup

1½ pounds young collard greens
4 strips bacon
3 tablespoons butter
½ cup chopped onions
1 green pepper, sliced
2 teaspoons chicken soup
concentrate

1 cup water
Milk and light cream
Salt and pepper

ACCOMPANIMENT
Buttered croutons

Trim the greens and put them in warm water in a dishpan. Warm water causes the grit from all greens to sink to the bottom of the pan; also it revives and freshens them. Rinse them well in cold water, drain, and cut in thin ribbons. Fry the bacon in the butter until crisp. Remove it, crumble, and set aside. Sauté the onion and green pepper in the fat until the onion begins to soften. Add the greens. Mix the soup concentrate with the water and add. Cover tightly and cook the greens until they are tender. (This takes 2½ minutes in a pressure cooker.) Purée the contents of the pot with milk and light cream to the consistency of heavy cream. Check the seasoning, it may need salt and pepper. We should use more chard and collard greens. Only in the South is their high food value fully appreciated. *Serves 6*

Corn Chowder

4 strips bacon, diced
2 tablespoons butter
1½ cups small cubes potatoes
1 cup finely diced onions
½ cup diced green pepper
Salt and pepper

2 cups fresh corn (4 ears)
2 cups warm chicken stock
1 tablespoon cornstarch
1 cup light or heavy cream
Milk

Fry the bacon in the butter until it is crisp. Remove the bacon crumbles and reserve. Put the vegetables in the fat and stir them a minute and add salt and pepper. Cover and cook 5 minutes over low heat until tender. Score each row of kernels with a sharp-pointed knife, then scrape the corn from the ears; this releases the milk. Add the corn to the vegetables, add the warm chicken stock, and simmer 1 minute; this is sufficient to cook the corn. Blend the cornstarch with the cream, bring to a boil, and add to the chowder. Add enough milk to thin to the right consistency. If fresh corn is not available, white shoepeg canned corn may be used. *Serves 6*

Cream of Fresh Corn Soup

3 cups fresh corn (5 or 6 ears)
1 cup warm milk
½ cup diced green pepper
4 tablespoons butter
1 teaspoon paprika
Salt and pepper
Milk

1 cup heavy cream
2 egg yolks

GARNISH

Browned sliced almonds, or
   chopped parsley, or paprika

Score the ears of corn down the center of each row of kernels with a sharp-pointed knife; this releases the milk. Scrape off the kernels and purée in a blender with 1 cup of warm milk, then sieve it. (The blender does not liquify the hard skin of the kernels.) Soften the onions and green pepper in the butter until tender, covered, purée with more warm milk, and add to the corn purée. Season with paprika, salt, and pepper. Add milk until the soup is the consistency of heavy cream. It should be very smooth. When ready to serve, reheat the soup. Scald the cream, mix it with the egg yolks, and whisk into the soup. The corn needs only to be brought to the boil before serving; this is sufficient cooking for fresh corn, especially when it has been puréed. If fresh corn is not available, use white shoepeg canned corn. Sprinkle each plate of soup with almonds or parsley or just with paprika. *Serves 6 to 8*

Potage Cressonière *(Cream of Watercress Soup)*
Paul Blanc, Chapon Fin, Thoissey, Ain

Everyone who has followed the gastronomy of France has heard of or visited Paul Blanc at Thoissey. The late Fernand Point wrote: "Paul Blanc est un des princes de la cuisine française."

1 large leek
¹/₃ cup butter
1¼ pounds potatoes, peeled and
   sliced
Salt
6 cups hot water

1 bunch watercress
½ cup thick cream

GARNISH

Watercress sprigs
Buttered croutons

Clean the leek and discard the coarse green part but use any tender with the white. Slice it very fine and soften it in the butter. Stir in the sliced potatoes, cook a moment, then add the salt and the hot water. Simmer gently 20 minutes. Wash the watercress and discard any thick stems. Save 6 sprigs for garnish and chop the rest fine in a wooden bowl. Add the chopped watercress to the soup and cook 5 minutes. Purée the contents of the pot. Reheat to serve and stir in the cream. Sometimes I use heavy cream mixed with sour cream to approximate the very thick cream of France, which has a slight tang. Garnish each plate of soup with a sprig of watercress and some buttered croutons. *Serves 6*

Cucumber Soup

3 cucumbers, peeled and diced	1 cup stemmed watercress or sorrel
3 slices bacon	Salt and pepper
1/3 cup butter	3 tablespoons wine vinegar
1 leek, sliced	6 cups hot chicken stock
1 white onion, diced	2 egg yolks

Peel the cucumbers and slice 1 inch thick, then quarter the slices. Sauté the bacon in the butter until crisp, remove, crumble, and reserve. Chop the watercress or sorrel very fine in a wooden bowl. Put the cucumbers, leek, onion, and watercress or sorrel in the fat and stir it with a wooden spoon 2 minutes over low heat. Add salt and pepper. Add the vinegar and hot stock and simmer gently 10 minutes, covered. Mix a little soup with the egg yolks, then whisk the mixture into the hot soup. Add the bacon. *Serves 6 to 8*

Cucumber and Potato Soup with Fresh Herbs

4 good-sized cucumbers	1/3 cup minced fresh herbs:
2 potatoes, peeled	tarragon, parsley, chives, thyme,
1/2 cup chopped onions	basil
6 cups water or chicken stock	Salt and freshly ground pepper

Peel the cucumbers and with a cutter make 24 little balls; 3 or 4 for each soup plate. Dice the rest of the cucumbers and the potatoes. Put them in a soup kettle with the water or stock. If water is used add 4 teaspoons chicken soup concentrate. Cover and simmer gently 10 minutes or until the potatoes are tender. Purée the contents of the pot, then add the minced herbs. Reheat the soup and serve in soup plates with the cucumber balls. *Serves 6 to 8*

Curly Chicory Soup

1 bunch chicory
Salted boiling water
4 tablespoons butter
¼ cup minced parsley
4 cups chicken broth
1 or 2 teaspoons curry powder

Salt and pepper
½ cup heavy cream
2 egg yolks

ACCOMPANIMENT

Croutons fried in butter

Trim a good-sized bunch of chicory, wash it, then cover with salted boiling water and let stand 5 minutes. Drain it and chop it fine in a wooden bowl. Melt the butter in a heavy pot, add the chicory and the parsley, and stir 2 minutes over low heat. Heat the broth with the curry and pour it over the greens; add salt and pepper to taste, cover, and simmer gently 10 minutes. Reheat the soup to serve. Scald the cream, mix it with the egg yolks, and whisk into the soup. *Serves 4 to 6*

Dandelion Soup

1¼ pounds dandelion greens
⅓ cup chopped onions
¼ cup chopped green pepper
4 tablespoons butter
⅓ cup water
3 cups chicken broth

1 cup light cream
Salt and pepper

GARNISH

Crisp buttered toast
Soft poached eggs

Trim and wash the greens; chop them a little. Fry the onions and green pepper in the butter until they soften, then stir in the greens with ⅓ cup water. Cover and cook until they are wilted, or for about 3 minutes. Purée the contents of the pot with the broth and cream. Season with salt and pepper. Reheat when ready to serve. Put a piece of toast in each soup plate, top with a soft poached egg, and pour the soup around it. *Serves 4 to 6*

Cream of Leek Soup

1 large bunch of leeks
⅓ cup butter
Salt and freshly ground pepper
1 tablespoon flour
6 cups hot chicken stock

1 cup heavy cream
2 egg yolks
2 tablespoons chopped parsley or
    chives

Quarter the leeks lengthwise. Wash them well and remove the coarsest green part but use as much of the green as possible. Slice them very fine because the soup is not sieved or puréed unless you wish a *velouté*. Put the leeks in a heavy pot with the butter and stir them 5 minutes over low heat; do not let them burn. Season and stir in the flour. Add the hot stock, cover, and simmer gently 15 minutes. When ready to serve, scald the cream, mix it with the egg yolks, and whisk into the hot soup. Do not boil again. Add the chopped chives or parsley. *Serves 8*

Leek and Potato Soup

1 bunch leeks
2½ cups water
Salt and pepper
⅓ cup butter
2 tablespoons oil
2 cups cubed peeled potatoes
2 teaspoons chicken soup
  concentrate

2 cups hot milk, or more
1 cup light cream
A few gratings of nutmeg
½ cup heavy cream
2 egg yolks

ACCOMPANIMENT

Bowl of grated Gruyère cheese

Wash the leeks, and slice very fine. Cook the green part 20 minutes in the 2½ cups of water. Sieve the leeks, pressing them against the sieve. Discard the leeks and save the water. Season the leek water. Put the butter and oil in a soup kettle, add the white part of the leeks, and stir until they begin to soften. Add the potatoes and the leek water. Cover and cook 15 minutes or until the vegetables are done. Dissolve the concentrate in 2 cups hot milk. Add it to the vegetables and mash through a coarse sieve. Add the light cream and nutmeg. If necessary, thin with more milk until the soup has the consistency of heavy cream. Reheat to serve. Scald the cream, mix it with the egg yolks, and whisk into the soup. Pass a bowl of cheese. *Serves 8*

Lettuce Soup

1 large head romaine lettuce
4 tablespoons ham fat or bacon fat
1 bunch green onions, or 3 white
   onions, sliced
Freshly ground pepper
Salt
1 teaspoon basil
1 teaspoon tarragon
½ cup water

4 cups chicken stock
1 cup heavy cream
1 teaspoon curry powder
1 teaspoon turmeric

GARNISH

Sliced hard-cooked eggs, or grated
   Parmesan cheese, or croutons
   fried in butter

Romaine has more flavor than some other lettuces and makes a very fine soup. Clean and trim the romaine and shred it quite fine on a wooden board. There should be 4 or 5 cups. Melt the fat in a heavy pot and soften the onions in it a moment, then add the lettuce, seasonings, herbs, and ½ cup water. Cover and steam 5 minutes over low heat. Add the stock. (If you lack stock use 4 cups of water and 2 tablespoons of chicken soup concentrate.) Mix well, then remove 2 tablespoons romaine and reserve. Purée the contents of the pot. Return the reserved lettuce to the purée. Heat the cream with the curry powder and turmeric. (If you don't have curry powder, ½ teaspoon each of anise, cumin, and caraway gives a lovely flavor.) Reheat the soup and add the hot cream. Serve in soup plates, adding your choices of the garnishes to each serving.

VARIATION: Chicken and Lettuce Soup. Purée 1 cup of diced chicken with an additional 1½ cups of chicken stock and add it to the soup. Julienne sticks of leftover chicken may be added to garnish it. *Serves 6 to 8*

Cream of Mushroom Soup
Ranieri, Rome

This restaurant was founded in 1843 and has been famous for well over a hundred years. Ranieri is not far from the Spanish Steps. The restaurant has kept an old-fashioned decor—three charming dining rooms, one gold, one red, and one olive green. Signor Nello Moranandi is the gracious host, whose chef serves this fine mushroom soup. The secret is that wild mushrooms are used which makes wonderful soup. This recipe is almost like Ranieri's and very good too.

5 to 6 cups rich chicken, beef, or
   game stock
1 cup Italian dried wild mushrooms

1 cup water
1 pound fresh cultivated
   mushrooms

¼ cup chopped onions
3 tablespoons butter
Salt and pepper

¼ teaspoon nutmeg
1 cup heavy cream
½ cup Madeira

This soup deserves a specially made stock of bones, meat, poultry carcass, vegetables, etc. Wash the dried mushrooms in boiling water and rinse them well. Soak them in 1 cup of water several hours or overnight. Clean the fresh mushrooms and slice them. Soften the onions in the butter in the top of a double boiler 1 minute. Add the fresh mushrooms and 1 cup of the stock, cover, and cook 20 minutes over simmering water. Drain the dried mushrooms, pressing them against the sieve. Add the soaking water to the stock. Chop the mushrooms very fine in a wooden bowl and cook them with 1 cup of stock 15 minutes, covered, in a heavy pot. Purée half the dried mushrooms and all the cooked fresh mushrooms in a blender. Season with a little salt and pepper. Rinse the blender with some of the stock. Combine the rest of the dried mushrooms with the purée and the rest of the stock. Add the nutmeg and the heavy cream. Reheat to serve, then add the wine. *Serves 8 to 10*

Duck Stock and Mushroom Soup

STOCK

Carcass of a roast duck
Giblets, dressing, and gravy (if
    available)
1 cup each chopped onions, carrots,
    and celery
1 leek, sliced
1 onion stuck with 2 whole cloves
Salt and pepper
1 cup dry white wine
8 cups water

3 teaspoons chicken soup
    concentrate

THE SOUP

1 pound fresh mushrooms
2 tablespoons lemon juice
4 tablespoons butter
3 tablespoons grated onion
1 cup heavy cream
2 egg yolks
½ cup Madeira

Make a stock with all the ingredients up to and including the soup concentrate. Cover and simmer 2 hours. Strain through a sieve. Clean the mushrooms and sprinkle them with the lemon juice. Put them in a heavy pan with the butter and grated onions and bake in a 350° oven 12 minutes. Chop half of them and purée the other half with their juices and 1 cup stock. Add both chopped and puréed mushrooms to the rest of the stock. When ready to serve, reheat the soup. Scald the cream, mix it with the egg yolks and whisk it into the soup. Add the wine and serve. Veal, beef, chicken, or turkey stock can also be used. *Serves 8*

Morel Mushroom Soup

1 cup dried morels, or 1 quart fresh
   morels
¼ cup butter
Salt and freshly ground pepper
2 tablespoons flour

6 or 7 cups hot rich chicken stock
1 cup heavy cream
2 egg yolks
1 jigger cognac

If you can find, receive, or otherwise obtain these precious fungi you are lucky. My father used to bring home quarts of them from the sandy banks of Nebraska's river Platte. If we had more fresh ones than we could eat, the rest were strung on lines in the attic to dry. They are also found in Ohio, Missouri, and New England. I have brought them from France at a price. Morels are always expensive because they are among the best and most sought after mushrooms in the world.

If you use dried morels, scald them in boiling water, rinse well, and soak a few hours in 1 cup or more of water, then drain and chop in a wooden bowl, and cook in the soaking liquid 15 minutes. Add a little salt and a few grinds of pepper. Mix the butter with the flour and add. Add the hot stock and let stand a few hours to ripen. Reheat to serve. Scald the cream, mix it with the egg yolks, whisk into the hot soup, and add the cognac.

If you use fresh morels, they must be thoroughly washed, as sand lurks in the many crevices of the caps and both caps and stems are hollow. Chop them fine in a wooden bowl and proceed as directed for dried morels, except that the fresh ones are cooked in 1 cup of stock. *Serves 6 to 8*

Okra Soup

6 cups chicken stock
¼ cup minute tapioca
½ to ¾ pound fresh small okra
1 pound fresh peas cooked with
   basil
1 small zucchini, sliced but not
   peeled

½ cup sliced green pepper
1 can white shoepeg corn
Salt and pepper
Dash cayenne
1 teaspoon turmeric

Put the stock in a heavy pot with the tapioca and simmer 15 minutes. Cook the vegetables separately. Cut off the tips of the okra, wash it in water with a pinch of soda, rinse well, and bring to a boil in fresh water. Cook 2 minutes, drain and add to the stock. Cook the peas in very little water with salt, pepper, and basil. Put them and their cooking liquid into the stock. Cook the zucchini and the green pepper, covered, for 5 minutes in ¼ cup of water over low heat. The corn needs no cooking. Add all the vegetables to the stock, just before the tapioca is done, and add the seasonings. Other fresh vegetables such as lima beans and green beans may be added. *Serves 8 to 10*

Cheese Onion Soup

1 pound onions, sliced thin	⅛ teaspoon nutmeg
¼ cup butter	¾ cup grated Gruyère cheese
2 tablespoons oil	6 slices French bread, toasted
Salt and pepper	½ cup soft Gorgonzola cheese
6 cups chicken or veal consommé	2 tablespoons heavy cream

Sauté the onions in the butter and oil until they soften. Season with salt and pepper and add the consommé and nutmeg. Simmer 2 minutes, then pass through a coarse sieve. Melt the Gruyère cheese in the soup and put the soup in an earthenware casserole. Toast the bread. Mix the Gorgonzola with the cream to a creamy spread. Spread it on the toast. Use more cheese if necessary to cover thickly. Put the toast on top of the casserole and bake in a 300° oven for 20 minutes. *Serves 6*

Onion Soup

1½ to 2 pounds Bermuda, yellow, or Italian red onions	2 quarts boiling rich beef broth
¼ cup butter	½ cup dry white wine
2 tablespoons oil	3 tablespoons brandy or Madeira
Salt and freshly ground pepper	
¼ teaspoon nutmeg	GARNISH
1 clove garlic, crushed	8 slices French bread, toasted
2 tablespoons flour	Shredded Swiss or Gruyère cheese

Slice the onions very fine and cook them in a heavy pot in the butter and oil for 20 minutes or until they soften; do not let them burn. Add the seasonings and garlic. Stir in the flour and when smooth add the boiling broth and wine. Cover and cook gently 25 minutes. This may be done in advance. When ready to serve, reheat the soup, add the brandy or Madeira, and pour the soup into an earthenware ovenproof tureen. Cover with toast and cover thickly with shredded cheese. Bake in a 500° oven until the cheese is golden. *Serves 8*

Le Thourin Bordelaise *(Bordeaux Onion Soup)*
Étienne Kraemer, Chef des Cuisines, S. S. *France*

½ pound onions, minced fine	Salt and freshly ground pepper
⅓ cup butter	
1 tablespoon flour	GARNISH
2 tablespoons tomato paste	6 slices French bread, toasted
6 to 7 cups boiling beef bouillon	Grated Gruyère cheese

Peel the onions, slice them, and cut each slice across into fine dice. Cook them slowly in a heavy pot in the butter without browning them, about 15 minutes. Stir in the flour and tomato paste. When the mixture is smooth stir in the boiling bouillon and season to taste. Simmer, covered, 10 minutes. Pour the soup into an earthenware ovenproof tureen. Put the toast over the top and cover thickly with grated Gruyère cheese. Bake in a 500° oven until the cheese is golden. *Serves 4 to 6*

For those who knew the *France* well, her passing leaves a happy but sad memory.   \

Soupe à l'Oignon Gratinée #1 *(Onion Soup au Gratin #1)*
Restaurant Allard, Paris

Mme. Fernande Allard is responsible for the Burgundian cooking in this popular bistro. André Allard inherited it from his father. The house dates back to the sixteenth century. It stands at the ancient crossroads of rue St. André des Artes and rue l'Eperon and was once a stagecoach stop.

5 large onions, sliced thin	Salt and pepper
3 tablespoons butter	
3 tablespoons oil	GARNISH
3 tablespoons flour	Grilled French bread
1 glass warm dry white wine	Grated Gruyère cheese
3 quarts boiling beef stock	

Cook the onions in a heavy pot over low heat, in the butter and oil, until onions are golden. Stir in the flour and when smooth and well-blended add the warm wine and the boiling bouillon. (Chicken broth may be used if you prefer). Cover and simmer slowly 1½ hours. Check the seasoning. Put the soup in an ovenproof tureen, cover with grilled French bread and cover thickly with grated cheese. Bake in a 450° oven about 10 minutes or until cheese is golden. *Serves 6 to 8*

Allard has a main-course specialty every day in the week. All are of special interest and high quality. It is hard to choose—it takes only six visits.

Soupe a l'Oignon Gratinée #2 *(Onion Soup au Gratin #2)*
Jean Dupin

Jean Dupin lives in Beaune and is one of France's finest printers, so it is only natural for him to be master of more than one art. I've been lucky enough to be on the receiving end of some of his dishes—among the best I have ever eaten.

This is a different onion soup, the only one not made with stock.

½-inch-thick slice salt pork	1 jigger cognac
½ cup butter	1 cup grated Gruyère cheese
3 pounds onions, sliced thin	1¼ cups heavy cream
3 tablespoons flour	2 egg yolks
2 cups dry croutons	
5 cups hot water	GARNISH
1 clove garlic, crushed	
1 cup dry white wine	**Buttered French bread**
	Grated Gruyère cheese

Dice the salt pork and fry it in ¼ cup of the butter until crisp. Scoop out the pork pieces. Add the rest of the butter to the pan and sauté the onions in it until they are yellow. Return the pork pieces to the pan and stir in the flour until smooth. Add the croutons, hot water, garlic, wine, and cognac. Cover and simmer gently 1 hour. Sieve the soup and cook 10 minutes, then add the cheese and when it is melted, sieve again. Scald the cream, mix it with the egg yolks, and whisk into the soup. Put the soup in an ovenproof tureen and cover with buttered bread; cover the bread thickly with the cheese. Bake in a 400° oven 10 minutes or until the cheese is golden. *Serves 8*

Soupe Soubise *(Cream of Onion Soup)*

2 pounds white onions
¹/₃ cup butter
2 tablespoons flour
4 cups boiling water
Salt and pepper
⅛ teaspoon powdered clove

1 cup heavy cream
2 egg yolks

ACCOMPANIMENTS

Buttered croutons
Bowl of grated Gruyère cheese

Slice the onions very fine. Sauté them in butter until they are yellow but not the least burned. Add the flour and stir until smooth, then add the boiling water, salt, pepper, and clove. Cover and cook 5 minutes. Purée the contents of the pot. This may be made in advance. When ready to serve, reheat the soup. Scald the cream, mix it with the egg yolks and whisk into the soup. Do not boil again. Serve with croutons or cheese. *Serves 6*

Soupe à l'Oignon avec Port *(Onion Soup with Port)*
Le Bossu, Lyon

Mme. Blanc's little restaurant is one of the best places in this gastronomic center to lunch or dine. Her chef makes an unusual and great onion soup. The fare is simple, which means French food at its best.

1½ to 2 pounds onions, sliced fine
¼ cup butter
2 tablespoons oil
Salt and pepper
¼ teaspoon nutmeg
1 clove garlic, crushed
2 tablespoons flour

2 quarts boiling rich beef consommé
1 wineglass port
2 egg yolks

GARNISH

Dried French bread
Grated Gruyère cheese

Sauté the onions in the butter and oil until they soften. Season with salt, pepper, and nutmeg. Add the flour and stir until smooth, then add the boiling consommé. Cover and simmer gently 45 minutes. This may be prepared in advance. When ready to serve, reheat the soup. Beat the wine and egg yolks in the bottom of an ovenproof tureen and pour in the boiling soup. Dry out the bread in the oven, put pieces all over the top of the soup, cover thickly with grated cheese. Bake in a 450° oven until cheese is golden, about 10 minutes. *Serves 8*

Parsley Soup

5 ounces parsley
1 bunch watercress
3 tablespoons butter
1¼ pounds potatoes, peeled and
   diced
¼ cup finely chopped onion
⅛ teaspoon nutmeg
Salt and pepper

2 tablespoons lemon juice
4 cups boiling water, or more
Big lump of butter

GARNISH

3 tablespoons chopped parsley
Buttered croutons

Wash and stem the parsley and watercress. Chop very fine in a wooden bowl. Soften a minute in a heavy pot with the 3 tablespoons butter, then stir in the potatoes and the onion. Cook a minute, then season with nutmeg, salt, pepper, and lemon juice. Add the boiling water, cover, and simmer gently 15 minutes. Purée the contents of the pot. Add more water to thin to heavy cream consistency. Reheat to serve and add the lump of butter. Stir in the chopped parsley and add crisp buttered croutons to the top of each plate of soup. If you prefer, remove 1 cup of soup and purée the rest, return the reserved cup of soup and reheat. This may also be served cold. *Serves 6*

Parsnip Soup

1¼ pounds small new parsnips
Salt and pepper
2 tablespoons butter
⅓ cup water
2 to 3 cups chicken broth
⅛ teaspoon mace or nutmeg
Milk to thin the soup

1 cup heavy cream
2 egg yolks
¼ cup rum or Madeira

GARNISH

Chopped parsley
Croutons fried in butter

Trim and scrub the parsnips. If they are young and ivory-colored they won't need scraping nor will they have a core to cut out. Slice them fine and put them in a heavy pot with salt, pepper, butter, and water. Cover and simmer gently until they are very tender (1½ minutes in the pressure cooker). Purée the contents of the pot with some of the broth. Add the rest of the broth to the purée with enough milk to obtain the consistency of heavy cream. Reheat to serve. Scald the cream, mix it with the egg yolks, and whisk into the soup. Add the rum or Madeira. Add the parsley and pass the croutons. This delicious soup is just the dish for those who don't like parsnips. *Serves 6*

Snow Pea Soup

1 pound snow peas	6 cups chicken stock
2 cups salted boiling water	2 tablespoons tapioca
2 teaspoons basil	½ cup cream (optional)

Wash and trim the peas. Boil them in the salted water in a soup pot until tender, about 15 minutes. Remove 2 cups of the peas, purée them with some of the chicken stock, return the purée to the pot, and add the rest of the stock. Cook the tapioca in the soup 15 minutes at a very low simmer. (If you prefer, cook the tapioca 15 minutes in 2 cups of the stock before you add it to the soup; this keeps the snow peas more crisp.) You may add ½ cup of cream if you like. *Serves 8*

Fresh-Pea Soup

3 pounds fresh peas	2 to 3 cups milk
5 white onions, sliced	1 cup light cream
¼ cup butter	¼ teaspoon nutmeg
2 teaspoons basil	
Salt and freshly ground pepper	GARNISH
⅔ cup water	Chopped fresh mint or parsley

Shell the peas—3 pounds should yield 3 cups. Sauté the onions in the butter until they begin to color, add the peas, basil, salt, pepper, and ⅔ cup of water. Cover and simmer gently 10 minutes. (A pressure cooker takes 1 minute.) Purée the contents of the pot with milk and use all the cream. The consistency should be like heavy cream. Add the nutmeg. This might be called the queen of soups. *Serves 8*

Pea Soup with Rice

½ cup Patna rice	2 teaspoons basil
2 cups vegetable juice	2 tablespoons butter
Salt and pepper	4 cups chicken consommé
½ cup chopped green onions	1 cup hot heavy cream
1½ to 2 pounds fresh peas	

Wash the rice and cook with the vegetable juice, salt, pepper, and green onions 25 minutes over low heat. Cook the peas with basil, salt, pepper, the butter, and ½ cup of water about 10 minutes in a heavy covered pot—(1 minute in a pressure cooker). Remove ½ cup of peas for garnish. Purée the rest with their cooking liquid and some of the consommé. Mix the purée with the rice. Add the hot heavy cream and enough consommé to make it soup consistency. Return the whole peas to the soup. *Serves 8*

Lettuce and Pea Soup

2 leeks, sliced
3 tablespoons butter
½ cup sliced celery
1 head Boston lettuce, shredded
2½ to 3 pounds fresh peas
1¼ cups boiling water
2 teaspoons basil or tarragon

Salt and freshly ground pepper
4 cups chicken broth or more
½ cup tiny noodle shells
Water
½ cup heavy cream
2 egg yolks

Cook the leeks in the butter in a soup kettle until they begin to color. Add the celery, lettuce, peas, boiling water, herb, salt, and pepper. Cover tightly and cook about 12 minutes. (A pressure cooker takes 1½ minutes.) Reserve ⅔ cup of the vegetables and purée the rest. Thin with the broth. Cook the noodle shells in boiling salted water until tender, drain, and add to the soup. Reheat when ready to serve. Return the reserved vegetables to the pot. Scald the cream, mix it with the egg yolks, and whisk into the soup. *Serves 10*

Potage Saint Germain *(Split-Pea Soup Saint Germain)*

2 cups dried split peas
6 cups water
1 cup chopped onions
½ cup chopped carrots
1 small white turnip, peeled and diced
2 tablespoons butter
1 stalk celery, sliced

1 teaspoon each chervil, basil, and tarragon
1 ham bone
Salt and pepper
1 cup hot heavy cream

GARNISH
1 cup cooked fresh peas (optional)

Wash the split peas and soak them 5 hours or overnight in the 6 cups of water. Put them in a large kettle with their soaking water and all the other ingredients except the salt, pepper, and cream. Cover and cook gently 1 hour. Remove the bone and purée the contents of the kettle. Check the seasoning. Reheat to serve and stir in the hot cream. The soup may also be made with a roast beef, lamb or pork bone. It may be garnished with a cup of cooked fresh peas. *Serves 6 to 8*

Baked Potato Soup

5 new potatoes
½ cup chopped onions
4 tablespoons butter
Salt and pepper
3 cups milk, or half milk and half
   chicken broth

½ cup heavy cream

GARNISH

Chopped chives

The soup may be made with freshly baked or leftover baked potatoes. Scrub the new potatoes, bring them to a boil, drain, and bake in a 350° oven until they are tender. The skins give the soup a good flavor. Slice the potatoes. Soften the onions in the butter until they begin to color then purée them with the potatoes and some milk, or part milk and part broth. Add more liquid to thin to the consistency of cream, then add the cream, reheat, and garnish with chives. *Serves 4 to 6*

Fresh Herb and Potato Soup

1 cup shredded lettuce
1 bunch watercress
4 ounces fresh spinach
4 ounces sorrel
2 tablespoons fresh tarragon
2 tablespoons fresh chervil
1 tablespoon fresh thyme
⅓ cup minced chives
2 leeks, sliced
¼ cup butter

2 tablespoons olive oil
3 cups boiling water
1½ pounds potatoes, peeled and
    diced
½ cup water
Salt and freshly ground pepper
3 cups hot chicken broth or more

ACCOMPANIMENT

Crisp buttered croutons

Wash the greens and trim off any bruised leaves or coarse stems. Chop the greens and herbs very fine in a wooden bowl (the soup is not puréed). Put the leeks with the butter and oil in a soup kettle and let soften a minute, then stir in the greens and herbs and cook another minute. Add the boiling water and let the greens steep. Boil the potatoes in ½ cup of water until they are tender. The water should be almost absorbed. Mash the potatoes through a coarse sieve into the greens and add the seasonings and 3 cups broth. Cook 5 minutes. If the soup is too thick add a little more hot broth. Pass buttered croutons.

VARIATION: Scald ½ cup of heavy cream, mix it with 2 egg yolks, and whisk into the hot soup. Do not boil again. *Serves 6*

Ham and Potato Soup

4 leeks, finely sliced	1 cup heavy sweet cream or sour
1/3 cup butter or bacon fat	cream
3 cups finely diced potatoes	1 cup ground cooked ham
5 to 6 cups hot chicken broth	3 tablespoons chopped parsley

Cook the leeks in the butter or fat until they begin to color, then stir in the potatoes. Cook 1 minute, then add the hot broth. Simmer 10 minutes and then mash the soup through a coarse sieve. (Most potato soups are better when mashed through a sieve so they remain a little grainy; if puréed the soup is too smooth and too much like a gravy.) Heat the cream, add the ham, put both in the bottom of a warm tureen, and pour in the hot soup. Mix in the parsley.

VARIATION: Sauté a cup of diced onion in butter and add 1½ pounds of sliced potatoes and 1 cup of water. Cook the vegetables until tender, thin with hot milk and light cream, and season with salt and pepper. Then mash the soup through a sieve. Chopped chives or chopped green onions are a popular garnish. *Serves 6 to 8*

La Soupe de Courge á la Créme
(Cream of Pumpkin Soup)
Paul Bocuse, Auberge du Pont de Collonges, Lyons

M. Bocuse says "The pumpkin is a neglected vegetable. It is good for gratins and for soups. Here is one that is both delicious and a novelty." The soup is made inside the pumpkin and it is a spectacular presentation when it is brought to the table and the soup served out of it.

12- or 13-pound pumpkin	5 cups light cream
5 slices homemade bread, toasted	Salt and pepper
½ pound shredded Gruyère cheese	½ teaspoon freshly grated nutmeg

Cut a round from the top of the pumpkin to serve as a lid. Remove all the pith and seeds from the inside. Fill the pumpkin by alternating the slices of toast with shredded cheese. Heat the cream with the seasonings and pour it into the pumpkin. Put on the lid; make sure it fits. Bake the pumpkin on a pan in a 325° oven 2½ hours. If it seems to be baking too fast, turn the oven to 300°. To serve, set the pumpkin on a tray, bring it to the table (of course as a surprise), remove the lid, scoop some of the flesh from the walls, and mix it with the soup. Serve in wide soup plates. *Serves 10 to 12*

A word of caution: the pumpkin must be young and firm. If it is old it may spring a leak and the precious liquid pour into the pan or oven. I know!

Pumpkin Soup

3 cups diced fresh pumpkin, or 2
   cups cooked mashed pumpkin
½ cup chopped onions
4 tablespoons butter
2 tablespoons brown sugar

½ teaspoon mace or nutmeg
Salt and pepper
4 to 5 cups chicken stock
1 cup heavy cream
¼ cup dark rum

If fresh pumpkin is used, steam it tender over ½ cup water. Soften the onions in the butter until they begin to color. Purée them with the pumpkin and seasonings and 1 cup of the stock until the purée is smooth, then thin with the rest of the stock. Add the cream, reheat the soup, and add the rum. This is good soup for Thanksgiving when you are not having pumpkin pie, as the recipe is easily increased. *Serves 6 to 8*

Cream of Salsify

1½ to 2 pounds salsify (oyster plant)
Cold water
Juice of 1 lemon
4 cups boiling water and 3
   teaspoons chicken soup
   concentrate or 4 cups chicken or
   veal stock
¼ cup chopped onions

1 teaspoon sugar
Salt and pepper
1 cup heavy cream
2 egg yolks

ACCOMPANIMENT

Buttered croutons

Peel or scrape the roots and drop them in cold water with half the lemon juice. This will prevent discoloring. Drain them. Slice them and add with the rest of the lemon juice to the water and concentrate, or the stock. Add the onions, cover, and cook until tender 7 to 12 minutes depending on the age of the salisfy. Purée with the liquid, adding a little more liquid if the mixture is too thick. Season to taste with sugar, salt, and pepper. Reheat to serve. Scald the cream, mix it with the egg yolks, and whisk into the soup. Do not boil again. Serve a bowl of buttered croutons. *Serves 6 to 8*

Potage Germiny *(Cream of Sorrel Soup)*
Maxim's, Paris

This soup is named for a nineteenth-century host, gourmet, and diplomat, Charles Gabriel Le Bèque, Comte de Germiny.

2½ cups sorrel leaves
3 tablespoons butter
6 cups rich, seasoned chicken or
   veal stock
1½ cups heavy cream

6 large egg yolks

ACCOMPANIMENT

Cheese straws (see index)

Wash and stem the sorrel. Chop it very fine in a wooden bowl. Melt the butter in the top of a double boiler and add the sorrel. Cover and cook 10 minutes over simmering water. The sorrel may or may not be puréed with a cup of the stock, as you choose. When the soup is ready to serve, heat the stock to boiling and pour it over the sorrel. Scald the cream, mix with the egg yolks, and pour slowly into the soup. Serve immediately. Cheese straws are a good accompaniment to this elegant soup. *Serves 8*

Breadcrumb and Sorrel Soup

½ pound sorrel
½ cup fine fresh breadcrumbs
¼ cup butter
Salt and pepper
1 teaspoon sugar

4 cups boiling water or veal or
   chicken stock
½ cup heavy cream
3 egg yolks
3 egg whites, beaten stiff

Wash and stem the sorrel. Put the crumbs in a wooden bowl, add the sorrel, and chop very fine. Soften the mixture over low heat in the butter, stirring it 1 or 2 minutes. Season with salt, pepper, and sugar. Add the boiling water or stock and simmer 15 minutes, covered. If water is used add 2 or 3 teaspoons chicken soup concentrate. Scald the cream, mix it with the egg yolks, and whisk into the hot soup. Do not boil again. Put the beaten egg whites into a warmed tureen and whisk the soup into them. When sorrel is not available, watercress and the juice of ½ lemon may be used.

VARIATION: Purée the soup, and add the cream. Beat 3 whole eggs until thick, and whisk into the soup. The soup may also be served cold with a garnish of chopped chives. *Serves 5 to 6*

French Squash Soup

4 leeks, sliced
5 tablespoons butter
6 cups hot veal or chicken stock, or more
1 cup chopped onions
½ cup chopped celery
3 cups diced Hubbard squash or acorn squash

Salt and pepper
1 tablespoon brown sugar
⅓ teaspoon nutmeg
1 cup heavy cream
2 egg yolks

GARNISH

Chopped chives or parsley

Cook the leeks in the butter until they begin to soften. Add the hot stock, the onions, celery, squash, and seasonings. Cover and cook gently 20 minutes, then purée the contents of the pot. Reheat to serve and thin the soup with a little stock if it is too thick. Scald the cream, mix it with the egg yolks, and whisk into the hot soup. *Makes 2 quarts of soup*

Alsatian Sauerkraut Soup

2 cups sauerkraut
½ cup chopped onions
2 or 3 tablespoons ham fat
1 cup Riesling wine
1 teaspoon powdered caraway
Freshly ground pepper
4 cups chicken stock
1 pound small pork sausages

ACCOMPANIMENT

3 knackwurst
Dijon mustard
Black bread
Riesling wine

Rinse the sauerkraut in hot water and drain it. (This should always be done before cooking sauerkraut to remove the harsh taste.) Sauté the onions in the fat until they color, and mix them with the sauerkraut. Add the wine, seasonings, and stock. Cover and simmer gently 20 minutes. Meanwhile brown the sausages in a 375° oven for 18 minutes. Boil the knackwurst 10 minutes. When the soup is done, add the sausages. Slice the knackwurst, spread with mustard, and serve along with the soup. *Serves 6*

Hungarian Sauerkraut Soup

1 pound smoked salt pork
2 quarts water
2 cups chopped onions
2 cloves garlic, crushed
3 cups blanched, rinsed sauerkraut
3 tablespoons butter
Hungarian sausage, sliced

2 tablespoons sweet Hungarian
  paprika
1 tablespoon flour
Salt and pepper
1 cup sour cream
1 cup cooked noodle shells
  (optional)

Rinse the smoked pork in boiling water. Put it in a soup kettle with 2 quarts fresh water, the onions, and garlic, and cook it, covered, 2 hours. Remove the pork, add the sauerkraut to the cooking water, and simmer it, covered, 10 minutes. Meanwhile slice and dice the pork, sauté it in a pan until golden, with the butter then add the sliced sausage, the paprika, and the flour and stir until mixture is smooth. When the sauerkraut has cooked 10 minutes, scrape in the pork and sausage mixture and cook 5 minutes. Check the seasoning. Reheat to serve and stir in the sour cream; add the noodles, if you like. Serves 6

Spinach Soup

1½ pounds fresh spinach
1 green pepper, sliced
1 large onion, sliced
3 tablespoons butter
1 teaspoon sugar
Salt and pepper

1 teaspoon each rosemary and basil
Milk and half-and-half

GARNISH

Croutons (optional)

Wash the spinach, first cutting off the roots and discarding any bruised leaves. Put it in a dishpan with quite warm water and let it stand 3 or 4 minutes so the grit sinks to the bottom of the pan. Warm water revives and freshens greens. Wash the spinach two more times, the last time in cold water. Drain it about 15 minutes in a lettuce basket. Put the green pepper and onions into a heavy pot in the butter and cook until they begin to soften. Put the spinach on top of the vegetables and add the seasonings and herbs. Cover tightly and cook 5 or more minutes over low heat until the spinach wilts. (A pressure cooker takes 30 or 40 seconds.) When cooking the spinach no water is added; there is enough clinging to the leaves if spinach is not drained more than 15 minutes. Purée the contents of the pot in a blender until smooth and creamy. Thin with milk and half-and-half until the consistency is like heavy cream. This is one of the most delicious soups and has a pure spinach taste. If you wish a richer flavor melt 2 or 3 teaspoons of chicken concentrate in the liquid just before the soup is put in the blender; ½ cup heavy cream may also be added. Buttered croutons may accompany the soup. *Serves 6 to 8*

Spinach and Sorrel Soup

Spinach and sorrel soup is made exactly like Spinach Soup, using ½ pound of sorrel and 1 pound of spinach. If you prefer, use 1 cup of chicken stock for thinning the soup when it is puréed. The French add sugar when cooking spinach and I must say it does improve the flavor. When other dishes do not exactly please, try a dash of sugar; it has rescued many a dish. *Serves 6 to 8*

Succotash Soup

This is a fine soup when the vegetables are fresh and young.

4 ounces salt pork	Salt and freshly ground pepper
3 tablespoons butter	1 pound fresh peas
²/₃ cup chopped onions	2 teaspoons basil
1 small green pepper, sliced	12 small okra
2 cups fresh corn, or 1 can white	²/₃ cup water
shoepeg corn	3 cups milk
1 pound fresh lima beans	1 cup heavy cream
2 teaspoons chervil	2 large egg yolks

Dice the salt pork and cook it with the butter in a soup kettle until it is crisp. Scoop out the pork pieces and reserve them. Cook the onions and green pepper in the fat until they soften. Turn off the heat. Add the other vegetables to the kettle as they are cooked. Score the corn down the center of the kernels, then scrape them from the ears into the kettle. If young corn is not available use the shoepeg corn and its liquid. Cook the lima beans with the chervil, salt and pepper, in very little water until tender. Add the beans and cooking water to the kettle. Do the same with the peas, basil, and salt and pepper and add to the kettle. Cut the tips from the okra and discard the tips, scald the okra and drain it. Cook it 5 minutes in ²/₃ cup of water, drain, and add to the kettle. Boil up the milk and pour it over the vegetables. This may stand an hour or more to ripen and blend the flavors. Add more salt and pepper if needed. When ready to serve, reheat the soup and add the reserved pork pieces. Scald the cream, mix it with the egg yolks, and add to the soup. Do not boil again. *Serves 8 to 10*

Sweet Potato, Pumpkin, or Squash Bisque

2 tablespoons butter
Salt and pepper
¼ teaspoon nutmeg
2 to 3 tablespoons honey or molasses
2 cups cooked, mashed sweet
    potato, pumpkin, Hubbard
    squash, or acorn squash

3 cups rich chicken broth
½ cup heavy cream
⅓ cup Madeira or 3 tablespoons
    dark rum

GARNISH

Sliced browned almonds or pecans

Mash the vegetables with the butter, seasonings, and the honey or molasses. Add the broth a little at a time and blend until smooth. Heat to serve, add the cream, and when hot add the wine or rum. Sprinkle a few nuts on top of each plate of soup.

VARIATION: To give a rich fruity flavor, sieve a big banana and add to the soup. This is especially good with pumpkin. Put 1 tablespoon dark rum in each soup plate before the soup is added. Add 2 halved chestnuts to each plate of soup if you wish; these may be fresh or drained chestnuts in syrup. A fine Thanksgiving soup. *Serves 6*

Cold Tomato Cream Soup

4 cups tomato juice
3 tablespoons grated onion
3 tablespoons grated celery
Salt and freshly ground pepper

1⅓ cups heavy cream

GARNISH

Avocado balls, or chopped chives

This is a delicious quick summer soup. Put 1 cup of the tomato juice in a blender and add the onion and celery. Purée until smooth. Season and whisk in the rest of the juice and the cream. Chill before serving. Garnish each soup plate with 4 avocado balls or with chopped chives. This soup may be frozen in an ice-cube tray to serve in gazpacho—2 cubes for each serving. *Serves 4*

French Tomato Soup

3 tablespoons butter
8 slices bacon, diced
1 cup chopped onions
2 cloves garlic, crushed
1 14½-ounce can small sliced
   tomatoes
1 teaspoon each fennel, basil, and
   chervil

Salt and freshly ground pepper
4 cups chicken stock
3 tablespoons flour
1 cup hot heavy cream
½ cup Madeira or port

Put the butter in a large saucepan and cook the diced bacon in it until it is crisp. Scoop out the bacon pieces and reserve them. Cook the onions and garlic in the fat over low heat until tender. Add the tomatoes, herbs, salt, and pepper and cook 5 minutes, covered. In another pan, blend the flour with a little of the stock, then add the rest of the stock and simmer 5 minutes. Add to the tomato mixture. All this may be done in advance. When ready to serve, reheat the soup, add the reserved bacon pieces, the hot cream, and the wine. *Serves 6 to 8*

Italian Fresh Tomato Soup

5 or 6 large ripe tomatoes, skinned
   and sliced
1 cup chopped onions
1 cup chopped celery
Salt and pepper
2 bay leaves

¾ cup scalded light cream

ACCOMPANIMENTS

Croutons fried in oil with fennel
   powder
Bowl of grated Parmesan cheese

Put the tomatoes, onions, celery, salt, pepper, and bay leaves in a pot and simmer gently 15 minutes. Strain through a sieve. Before serving reheat the soup and stir in the scalded cream. Pass bowls of croutons and cheese. The beauty of this soup is its fresh taste. It must be made with real home-grown tomatoes. In winter use a large can of plum tomatoes. *Serves 6 to 8*

Jean Dupin's Tomato Soup

Another recipe from this famous printer. Jean Dupin prints Burgundy's most beautiful wine labels as well as the lovely menus for the Hotel de la Poste in Beaune.

6 large ripe tomatoes, skinned and
  sliced
1/3 cup melted butter
1½ cups dry croutons, ½-inch size
Salt and freshly ground pepper
3 cloves garlic, crushed

6 cups hot water
1½ cups heavy cream
2 egg yolks

ACCOMPANIMENT

Croutons fried in butter

Skin the tomatoes and slice them into the butter in a soup kettle. Stir 3 or 4 minutes over low heat. Stir in the dry croutons, salt, pepper, and garlic. Add the hot water and simmer gently, covered, 1 hour. Sieve the soup, return to the kettle, cover, and cook gently 1 more hour. Sieve again. Scald the cream, mix it with the egg yolks, and whisk into the hot soup. Do not boil again. Serve with fried croutons. *Serves 6*

Near East Tomato Soup

1½ cups tomato purée
2 tablespoons minced parsley
½ cup diced celery or celery root
½ cup diced onions
1 or 2 teaspoons cumin or caraway
  powder

5 cups lamb or chicken stock
3 tablespoons semolina (cream of
  wheat)
2 tablespoons capers

Put all the ingredients except the semolina and capers in a heavy pot. Simmer, covered, 10 minutes, then purée the contents of the pot. Check the seasoning; salt and pepper may be needed if the stock is not well seasoned. If lamb stock is used the fat must be removed before cooking with the vegetables. Add the semolina and simmer 10 minutes more. Add the capers. *Serves 6 to 7*

Tomato and Potato Soup

1 quart ripe tomatoes, skinned and
  sliced, or 1 quart can tomatoes in
  purée
½ cup fresh breadcrumbs
1½ pounds potatoes, peeled and
  diced
6 cups boiling water
2 tablespoons chicken soup
  concentrate
½ cup chopped onions

2 teaspoons fennel powder or thyme
  and basil
Salt and pepper
2 tablespoons brown sugar
¼ cup butter

GARNISH

Sour cream
Buttered croutons

Unless you can get home-grown tomatoes, it is better to use a good brand of tomatoes canned in purée than to use hot-house tomatoes. Put all the ingredients except the butter in a heavy pot. Cover and simmer gently 20 minutes. Purée the contents of the pot and add the butter. A blob of sour cream on top of each plate of soup is a good addition. Pass croutons. *Makes over 2 quarts*

Tomato and Vegetable Soup

2 pounds tomatoes, skinned and
  sliced, or 1 quart can tomatoes in
  purée
1 cup chopped onions
2 green peppers, sliced
2 cloves garlic, crushed
¼ cup minced parsley
2 tablespoons brown sugar
1 cup sliced carrots
1 teaspoon thyme

1 teaspoon fennel
Salt and pepper
¼ cup butter
¼ cup oil
1 quart tomato juice or vegetable
  juice

GARNISH

Sour cream or croutons

Put all the ingredients except the juice in a heavy pot. Cover and simmer 10 minutes, then add the juice and cook 10 minutes more. Purée the contents of the pot. Reheat and serve with a bowl of sour cream or croutons. *Makes over 2 quarts*

Tomato Bouillon

This fine bouillon has many uses in addition to serving as is with cheese straws, a bowl of cheese, or crisp croutons fried in butter. It may be the base of the other soups, or cooked noodle shells and a cup of cooked peas may be added before serving. It keeps well in glass screw-top jars in the refrigerator.

2 large cans tomatoes in purée
1 large can vegetable juice
1 12-ounce can carrot juice
½ cup chopped celery and leaves
½ teaspoon powdered clove
½ cup chopped onions
¼ cup minced parsley

2 teaspoons brown sugar
Salt, pepper, and cayenne to taste
2 to 3 cups strong beef stock

ACCOMPANIMENTS

Bowls of croutons and grated cheese

Put all the ingredients except the stock in a large kettle, cover, and simmer 15 minutes. Strain the contents of the kettle. If the beef stock is not homemade, use boiling water and beef glaze and beef soup concentrate. The stock should have a strong flavor. Add the stock to the strained soup and simmer gently 10 minutes, covered. *Makes 3½ quarts*

This bouillon makes a fine aspic ring to fill with cooked vegetables or fresh fruits. For every pint of liquid, soak 1 tablespoon of commercial gelatin in lemon juice or in ½ cup of Madeira and then melt it in a little hot bouillon.

Cream of White Turnip Soup

1½ pounds new small white
    turnips, peeled and diced
½ cup chopped onions
1 large potato, peeled and diced
⅓ cup butter
Salt and pepper
5 to 6 cups chicken stock

¼ teaspoon nutmeg
1 cup heavy cream
2 egg yolks

ACCOMPANIMENT

Grated Gruyère cheese or buttered
    croutons

Dice the vegetables very fine. Put them in the butter in a heavy pot with a little of the broth and salt and pepper and stir until they are tender. Purée half the vegetables with some of the broth, then combine the purée with the rest of the broth and vegetables. Add the nutmeg. When ready to serve, reheat the soup, scald the cream, mix it with the egg yolks, and whisk into the hot soup. Pass a bowl of cheese to sprinkle on top of the soup or serve buttered croutons. *Serves 8*

Vichyssoise

5 or 6 leeks (white part only), sliced
   fine
⅓ cup butter
4 medium-sized potatoes, diced fine
½ cup boiling water
Salt and pepper

5 cups rich chicken consommé
1 cup heavy sweet cream, mixed
   with 1 cup sour cream

GARNISH

½ cup chopped chives

Slice the leeks very fine and soften them 2 or 3 minutes in the butter, stirring them continuously so they do not color. Add the potatoes and stir them a minute with the leeks. Add ½ cup of boiling water, cover tightly, and simmer gently until the leeks and potatoes are very soft. Add salt and pepper and mash through a sieve with the consommé. You may put the soup through a blender, but some prefer a slight grainy quality. The soup should be very smooth and blended well with the consommé. Cool and chill in the refrigerator. This can be made ahead of time and stored in an earthenware or glass bowl. Before serving, stir the cream mixture until well blended, then stir into the soup. Put the cold soup in soup plates or bowls and sprinkle each serving with chives. *Serves 8*

Watercress Soup

1 large bunch watercress
2 white onions, diced
1 large potato, peeled and diced
4 tablespoons butter
3 to 4 cups hot chicken consommé

Salt and pepper

GARNISH

Sprigs of watercress
Buttered croutons

Trim and wash the watercress, removing any very coarse stems; the tender stems are used. Drain in a salad basket. Reserve 8 sprigs for garnish and chop the rest of the watercress very fine in a wooden bowl. Soften the onions and potato in the butter in a soup kettle 1 minute, then add the watercress and moisten with the hot consommé. Cover and simmer 15 minutes. Remove ½ cup of the soup and purée the rest. Return the ½ cup of soup to the purée. Reheat the soup. Garnish each soup plate with a sprig of watercress. Serve a bowl of croutons.

VARIATION: Mix ⅓ cup heavy cream with ⅓ cup of sour cream. When the soup is reheated to serve, stir in the cream mixture. *Serves 4 to 6*

Potage Chaumière *(Vegetable Soup)*
La Chaumière, Paris

This fine neighborhood restaurant has been our standby for many years and has a large, devoted clientele that evidently shares our feeling. It is friendly and homelike and is one of "The Hundred," which is a great honor in Paris. M. and Mme. Richard are the hosts; chef Andrillon gave me this recipe.

1½ pounds potatoes, diced	⅓ cup butter
4 young carrots, diced	2 tablespoons oil
4 white turnips, peeled and diced	2 quarts boiling beef or chicken
2 leeks, sliced fine	consommé
½ cup sliced celery	Salt and pepper
1 cup diced onions	1½ cups small cubes boiled beef

Stir all the vegetables in the butter and oil over low heat 3 or 4 minutes. Do not brown them. Add the boiling consommé, cover, and simmer gently 25 minutes. Add salt and pepper and the boiled beef and serve in a marmite or tureen. *Serves 8*

Potage Forestière *(Mixed Vegetable Soup)*

½ cup carrots, cut in julienne sticks	4 ounces fresh mushrooms
½ cup white turnips, peeled and cut in julienne sticks	3 tablespoons butter
	¼ cup vermicelli
½ cup thinly sliced leeks	½ cup heavy cream
½ cup sliced green onions	3 tablespoons chopped parsley or
3 tablespoons butter	minced fresh tarragon leaves
6 cups boiling chicken consommé	

The vegetables are cut quite fine. Put all in a heavy pot with 3 tablespoons butter, cover tightly, and steam over low heat, shaking the pot several times to prevent burning. Add the boiling consommé, cover and cook gently. Meanwhile sauté the sliced mushrooms a minute in the other 3 tablespoons butter. Add the mushrooms and the vermicelli to the soup and cook, covered, 15 minutes. Stir in the heavy cream and the herb. If you can get fresh tarragon it makes a fragrant soup. *Serves 6 to 8*

Czech Vegetable Soup with Dill

1½ tablespoons flour
1½ cups heavy cream
3 tablespoons vinegar
½ cup finely chopped fresh dill
Salt and pepper
1 teaspoon basil
1 pound fresh peas

1 cup green beans cut in ½-inch
   lengths
1½ cups cubed potatoes
2 tablespoons butter
1 cup water
6 soft poached eggs
Paprika

Blend the flour with a little of the cream until smooth, then add the rest of the cream. Bring to a boil, stirring continuously. Add the vinegar and dill. Add salt and pepper. Let this mixture stand 1 hour. Put the basil, peas, beans, potatoes, butter, and 1 cup of water in a heavy pot, cover, and cook until the vegetables are done. Do not drain. Combine with the cream mixture. Serve the soup in hot wide soup plates and top each serving with a soft poached egg. Sprinkle the tops of the eggs with paprika. This is an unusual and delicious soup. *Serves 6*

Crème de Lègumes *(Cream of Vegetable Soup)*
Le Bossu, Lyons

3 medium-sized potatoes, peeled
   and diced
4 leeks, sliced
3 young carrots, sliced
3 ripe tomatoes, skinned and sliced
Salt and pepper

4 cups water
⅓ cup heavy cream
1 egg yolk

ACCOMPANIMENT

Buttered croutons

Prepare the vegetables, season, and cook gently in the water 1 hour. Purée the contents of the pot. Reheat to serve. Scald the cream, mix it with the egg yolks, and whisk into the soup. Serve with buttered croutons. *Serves 6 to 8*

Herb Gardeners' Soup

⅔ closely packed cups chopped
   fresh herbs: tarragon, thyme,
   chervil, basil, savory
¼ cup butter
4 cups boiling chicken consommé or
   water and chicken soup
   concentrate
Salt

Pepper
1 teaspoon sugar
2 eggs, beaten
3 tablespoons minced fresh tarragon

ACCOMPANIMENT

Buttered croutons

Chop the herbs fine in a wooden bowl. Heat the butter and stir the herbs in it 2 minutes. Then add the boiling consommé or water. (If water is used, add 3 teaspoons chicken soup concentrate.) Skimp the salt. Add pepper and the sugar. Simmer gently 10 minutes. Beat the eggs in a warm tureen until thick, then stir in the 3 tablespoons fresh tarragon for extra perfume. Whisk the boiling soup into the egg mixture. Serve with buttered croutons. *Serves 4*

Cream of Fresh Herbs

This fragrant soup is dedicated to those who are blessed with a herb and vegetable garden. The greens are finely chopped and shredded because the soup is not strained. Never grind them but mince and chop in a wooden bowl with a double-bladed chopper.

1/3 cup butter
1 cup finely shredded romaine
   lettuce
1 cup finely chopped watercress or
   spinach
1 cup finely chopped sorrel
1 tablespoon each minced tarragon,
   chervil, and parsley
2 teaspoons sugar

6 cups boiling rich chicken broth or
   more
Salt and pepper
1 cup heavy cream
2 egg yolks

ACCOMPANIMENT

Small croutons fried in butter

Melt the butter in the top of a double boiler and add the greens, herbs, and sugar. Cover and cook 10 minutes over simmering water. Pour the boiling broth over the herbs, remove from heat, partly cover, and let stand several hours to infuse. When ready to serve, check the seasoning and bring the soup to a boil over direct heat. Scald the cream, mix with the egg yolks and whisk into the soup. Pass a bowl of croutons or sprinkle some over each cup or plate of soup. *Serves 6 to 8, depending on the amount of broth*

Spring Vegetable Soup

1 pound potatoes, peeled and diced
  fine
2 young carrots, thinly sliced
2 cups water
Salt and pepper
2 bunches green onions, thinly
  sliced
1 cup finely shredded lettuce
¼ cup butter

2 tablespoons oil
4 cups chicken broth
1 cup fresh peas
1 teaspoon basil
²/₃ cup heavy cream, scalded
2 egg yolks

GARNISH

Minced chives

Put the potatoes, carrots, and water in a heavy pot, add some salt and pepper, and cook, covered, until the vegetables are tender, then purée them with their cooking water. Soften the green onions and the shredded lettuce in the butter and oil for 3 minutes. Empty them into the purée. Mix in the chicken broth. Cook the peas in very little water with the basil and a little salt. Add them to the soup; if it is too thick add a little more broth. Before serving, reheat the soup. Scald the cream, add it to the egg yolks, and whisk into the soup. Do not boil again. Sprinkle each serving with chives. This is a lovely soup to make with new vegetables. *Serves 8*

Mathilde's Special Vegetable Soup

¹/₃ cup butter
2 leeks, sliced
1 onion, minced
6 ounces mushrooms, sliced
2 tablespoons flour
Salt, pepper, paprika
2 quarts hot chicken consomme
2 ripe tomatoes, skinned and
  chopped

3 tablespoons rice
½ cup heavy cream

GARNISH

½ cup each cooked peas, green
  beans, carrot balls, and button
  mushrooms

Put the leeks, onion, and mushrooms in the butter in a good-sized pot and stir 2 minutes, then add the flour, stir until smooth and add the seasonings. Add the hot consommé, the tomatoes, and the rice. Cover and simmer gently 20 minutes. Purée the contents in a blender and add the cream. Cook all the garnish vegetables in a heavy pot with 2 tablespoons butter and 2 or 3 tablespoons water. The peas take 8 or 10 minutes over low heat, covered; so do the beans, cut in ½-inch lengths, and the carrots. (A pressure cooker takes one-fourth the time.) The mushrooms take 2 minutes. Before serving reheat the soup and add the garnishes. *Serves 8*

Fruit Soups

Serving Fruit Soups

When to have fruit soup? What to serve with it? For a summer lunch, a cold fruit soup with a delicious hot bread and a custard cream or zabaglione for dessert makes a balanced meal. Serve a Vouvray before and during lunch. Rita, who gave me the recipe for Scandinavian Fruit Soup, says her father likes this soup with pancakes in the winter.

Rita's Scandinavian Fruit Soup

1 cup dried apricots	1/3 cup light brown sugar
5 cups water	3 or 4 sticks cinnamon
1 cup ready-to-eat pitted prunes	1 cup diced tart apple
1/3 cup seedless raisins	1 cup white wine
A few grains of salt	3 tablespoons minute tapioca

Wash the apricots and soak them in the water 30 minutes. Add the prunes, raisins, salt, sugar, and cinnamon, cover, and simmer gently 15 minutes. Remove the cinnamon sticks and add the apple, wine, and tapioca. Simmer, covered, 8 minutes more. Some boil paper-thin slices of lemon with the prunes; I happen to prefer prunes without lemon. Serve hot or cold in cups. You may vary the fruits, using fresh peaches and plums when in season, instead of the dried fruits. *Serves 7 to 8*

Beet and Fruit Soup

8 new beets	1 tablespoon honey or brown sugar
2 cups water	1 cup dry red wine
3/4 teaspoon powdered clove	
Salt and pepper	GARNISH
Juice of 2 lemons or limes	
Frozen grape juice concentrate, diluted with 1½ cans water	Pitted fresh cherries or canned Bing cherries
Grapefruit juice	Sour cream (optional)

This is a beautiful soup, with the clove and grape juice giving it a fascinating flavor. Wash the beets well because their cooking water is used in the soup. Cut the stems a good inch from the beets. Cook them in the 2 cups water until tender. Small beets take about 18 minutes; large beets take much longer. Drain, saving the water. Skin the beets, slice them into a blender, and purée with all the seasonings and some of the juices. Add the wine. Thin the soup with more grapefruit juice to the consistency of heavy cream. When fresh beets are not available, use a good brand of canned whole beets. This is equally good hot or cold. Garnish with fruit and add a small blob of sour cream to each serving if desired. The soup keeps very well in screw-topped glass jars in the refrigerator. *Makes over 2 quarts*

Blender Fruit Soups for Children

CHOICE OF FRUITS

Bananas, peaches, apricots, strawberries, raspberries

LIQUIDS

Orange juice, grape juice, grapefruit juice, pineapple juice
Milk or half-and-half

Egg yolks

GARNISH

Melon balls, whole berries, cherries, balls of ice cream

Any fresh fruit or combination of fruits or fresh or frozen strawberries or raspberries may be sliced into a blender and puréed with any of the liquids to a creamy smoothness. The addition of raw egg yolks (omit the whites) makes the soup, plus a sandwich, a nourishing lunch for small children. In summer a ball of ice cream may be added to each soup plate. The combinations are endless. Add powdered coconut to pineapple juice for a divine drink. Some old children also like these combinations, perhaps with a spot of rum. If raspberries are used, sieve after puréeing.

Cantaloupe or Honeydew Soup

3 cups sliced ripe cantaloupe or honeydew melon
2 tablespoons butter
¼ teaspoon nutmeg
1½ cups strained fresh grapefruit juice
Juice of 2 limes
2 tablespoons honey

Salt and pepper to taste
¼ cup heavy cream
1 or 2 jiggers Cointreau or Curaçao

GARNISH

18 Melon balls marinated in ⅓ cup light rum

First marinate the melon balls for the garnish in ⅓ cup of rum 1 hour in the refrigerator. Sauté the sliced melon in the butter and nutmeg 2 minutes over low heat, then purée it with the juices and seasonings. After it is puréed, whisk in the cream and liqueur. Chill. When ready to serve, put 3 melon balls in each soup plate, add the rum to the soup, and serve. *Serves 6*

Carrot and Orange Soup

2 bunches new carrots
¼ cup butter
Salt and pepper
½ cup chopped onions
3 to 4 cups orange juice
1 can carrot juice
⅛ teaspoon mace or nutmeg

Juice of 1 lemon or lime (optional)
½ cup heavy cream (optional)

GARNISH

Chives, parsley, or fresh mint, or
  berries, pitted cherries, melon
  balls, or avocado balls

Scrub the carrots, slice them, and stir them in the butter with the seasonings and onions 1 minute over low heat, then add 1 cup orange juice, cover, and cook until carrots are tender (the pressure cooker takes 3 minutes). Purée the mixture with more orange juice and the carrot juice and spice. If it is too sweet for your taste, add the lemon or lime juice. Add enough orange juice to obtain the consistency of cream. Add the heavy cream if desired. This soup is especially liked by children when it is garnished with fruit. Serve cold or hot. *Serves 6 to 8*

Cold Buttermilk Soup or Drink

This was served to me at a garden lunch with hot blueberry muffins—a lovely combination.

6 cups buttermilk
1 teaspoon cinnamon
1 teaspoon nutmeg, freshly grated
Grated rind of 2 lemons

4 to 5 tablespoons lemon juice
⅓ cup powdered sugar
1½ cups heavy cream, whipped

Whip the buttermilk with a rotary beater until it is very frothy. Beat in the seasonings, then blend in the whipped cream. Chill. This should be served very cold and is most refreshing in summer. It has the flavor of lemon sherbet. *Serves 6 as soup or as a beverage*

Fruit Soup

1 pound black cherries, pitted
2 or 3 fine peaches, skinned and
  sliced
1 stick cinnamon
4 whole cloves
Juice of 1 lime
4 cups grapefruit juice
3 tablespoons honey

2 tablespoons cornstarch
2 or 3 tablespoons cold water
1 teaspoon almond extract
1 cup claret or sauterne

GARNISH (optional)

Sour cream or slivered browned
  almonds

Put the fruit in a saucepan. Tie the cinnamon stick and cloves in a cheesecloth bag and add to the fruit with the lime juice, grapefruit juice, and honey. Cover and simmer 5 minutes. The fruit should not become mushy. Remove the spice bag. Blend the cornstarch with 2 or 3 tablespoons cold water, stir into the soup, and cook until the soup is clear—2 or 3 minutes. Cool and chill the soup. Just before serving add the almond extract and the wine. A small blob of sour cream, or a few slivered browned almonds may be put on top of each plate of soup. See that each serving contains cherries and peaches. *Serves 8*

Cherry Soup *(Limousin)*

1½ pounds cherries, pitted
3 cups water
3 cups grapefruit juice
A few grains salt

Grated rind of 1 lemon
3 eggs
¼ cup light brown sugar
1 cup white wine

Simmer the cherries, liquid, salt, and grated rind 20 minutes over low heat. Beat the eggs until thick, then beat in the sugar until mixture is creamy. Pour the boiling soup into the mixture and let cool. When cool add the wine and chill the soup. Serve in cups. *Serves 8*

Fruit and Tomato Consommé

4 cups tomato juice or vegetable
  juice
1 cup orange juice
1 cup grapefruit juice
Salt and pepper (optional)

GARNISH

Chopped chives, mint, or parsley
Melon or avocado balls
Crisp croutons

This is a flexible soup and the proportions may be varied to suit your taste. Season with salt and pepper if you like. Serve hot or cold in cups, with any of the garnishes. *Serves 6*

Rhubarb Soup

1 pound pink rhubarb
3 cups orange juice
1½ tablespoons cornstarch
2 tablespoons cold water

1 cup sauterne

GARNISH

Melon balls or pitted cherries

Hothouse rhubarb makes a prettier soup. Trim and wash the rhubarb and cut in ½-inch slices—this prevents it from interfering with the blender knives. Cook it 5 minutes in 1 cup of the orange juice and season to taste with honey. Purée it in a blender with the rest of the orange juice. Blend the cornstarch with the cold water and add to the soup. Cook until the soup is clear—2 minutes. Chill. Before serving, stir in the wine. Garnish each plate of soup with 4 or 5 melon balls or cherries.

VARIATION: Gooseberry soup may be made the same way. Serves 4 or 5

Accompaniments, Garnishes, Sauces, and Thickeners

Cheese Straws

6½ tablespoons grated Parmesan
   cheese
½ cup sweet butter softened to room
   temperature

½ cup sifted flour
¼ teaspoon dry mustard

Mix the cheese with the softened butter. Mix the flour with the mustard and cut in the butter mixture as you would for pie crust. Wrap the dough in wax paper and chill several hours. Roll out ⅓-inch thick and cut in sticks ⅓-inch wide and 4 inches long. Bake at 375° on a cookie sheet until the straws are golden. Serve to accompany soup. *Serves 6 or 8*

Gnocchi Spinaci *(Spinach Gnocchi)*

¾ pound fresh spinach
2 tablespoons butter
5½ ounces grated Parmesan cheese
1¾ cups fresh breadcrumbs
2 extra-large eggs

1 cup plus 3 tablespoons sifted flour
2 potatoes, boiled and sieved
Salt and pepper
⅛ teaspoon nutmeg
Boiling salted water

Trim the spinach and wash in warm water, drain, and wash twice more in cold water. Drain an hour in a salad basket. Chop very fine and press against a sieve to remove some of the water. Soften in the butter 1 minute then press again against a sieve to drain. Mix with all the other ingredients. Roll small amounts at a time into 1-inch tubes, then cut in ¾-inch lengths. Put them in a heavy pan, carefully add boiling salted water, bring to a boil, and drain immediately. Cool and refrigerate. Before serving, bring them to room temperature, and warm in butter, sauce, or soup to serve, no further cooking is needed. They are delicate and tender. Serve 4 in each plate of soup. They also may be warmed in butter and served as a pasta. *Serves 6 to 8 as a pasta*

Preparing Fresh Spinach for Soups

In some soups, particularly lentil, white bean, lima bean, and split pea soups, fresh spinach is an unusual and excellent addition. The spinach is washed, cooked, and puréed separately from the soup to which it is added. It gives a fresh, herby, and fascinating flavor. A pound of spinach is a good proportion for a quart of the soup. This recipe can be divided for other soups and lesser amounts.

1 pound fresh spinach	1½ tablespoons butter
½ cup chopped onion	2 teaspoons dried basil, rosemary,
1½ tablespoons oil	or powdered fennel

Wash the spinach thoroughly, first in quite warm water and then in cold. Drain in a colander a short time so very little water is added when it is cooked. The pressure cooker is ideal for cooking green vegetables. Sauté the onions in the butter and oil in the bottom of a pot until the onions begin to soften, then add the spinach and herbs. The pot is put over low heat to begin the cooking, then the heat is increased. When the steam comes up turn down the heat; the spinach will be done in 2 minutes. Purée the spinach in the electric blender. Add salt and pepper to taste. The spinach is now ready to be added to the puréed soup.

Liver Quenelles

¼ cup chopped onions	½ teaspoon thyme
2 tablespoons butter	¼ teaspoon nutmeg
4 ounces calf's liver or pork liver	½ cup breadcrumbs
1 tablespoon minced parsley	¼ cup sifted flour
1 egg, beaten	Hot consommé
Salt and pepper	

Soften the onions in the butter and grind with the liver, using a fine blade. Mix all the ingredients except the consommé together and form into tiny dumplings. Roll them lightly in flour and boil 3 or 4 minutes in simmering consommé, covered. Serve 4 in each plate of soup. *Makes about 2 dozen*

Meat Quenelles

2½ ounces ground beef or veal	Salt and pepper
2½ ounces ground pork	2 tablespoons cream
2 tablespoons grated onion	¼ cup fine breadcrumbs
1 tablespoon butter	Flour
1 egg yolk	Broth or butter for cooking

Mix the meats together. Soften the onion in the butter a few seconds. Mix together all the ingredients except the flour, make little balls and roll them in flour. Poach them in broth 5 minutes, or fry in butter until lightly browned. Put 3 or 4 in each plate of soup. *Makes 18 to 24*

Italian Soup Balls for Consommé or Tomato Soup
(Zuppa Incantata)

This old Italian family recipe comes from Nice Ugolotti-Serventi, a friend from Parma.

2 eggs, beaten	2 ounces Mortadella sausage,
²/3 cup breadcrumbs	ground
²/3 cup grated cheese	Boiling salted water
Salt and pepper	
1 teaspoon powdered fennel or oregano	

Beat the eggs until light, then mix them with all the other ingredients. If Mortadella is not available, squeeze any other good pork sausage from the casing. Make a small ball of the mixture and put it in boiling salted water; if it does not hold together add 2 tablespoons more crumbs. Shape the mixture into little balls. Boil half of them at a time in boiling salted water, 15 minutes, covered. They will puff up. Cook these ahead of time and drain. At the moment of serving add 5 or 6 to each plate of hot soup. *Makes about 40*

Sausage Balls for Soup

3 tablespoons butter	2 large eggs
1/3 cup hot water	1/3 cup ground sausage or salami
²/3 cup sifted flour	Oil for deep frying
Salt	
2 tablespoons grated Parmesan cheese	

Put the butter and hot water in a saucepan over medium heat and when the butter is melted stir in the flour. Stir until the dough leaves the sides of the pan, remove from heat, and add a little salt, and the cheese. When the cheese is melted beat in the eggs, 1 at a time. Add the sausage or salami. Form the mixture into little balls. Deep-fry at 370° until golden, drain on brown paper. Serve in beef or chicken consommé. *Makes 24*

Profiteroles *(Cream Puff Paste)*

PÂTE À CHOU

¼ **cup butter**
½ **cup milk**
¼ **teaspoon salt**
½ **teaspoon sugar**

⅞ **cup sifted flour**
3 **eggs**

FILLING

Mornay sauce

Make a pâte à chou by melting the butter in the milk and adding the salt, sugar, and flour all at once. Stir the mixture until it leaves the sides of the saucepan. Preheat the oven at 400°. Let the paste cool a minute, then beat in the eggs, 1 at a time. Put the mixture by teaspoonfuls on a greased baking sheet and bake 20 minutes. When the puffs are taken from the oven, make a slit on the side of each to release the steam. If they aren't golden in color, let them dry out in the oven with the heat turned off and the oven door propped open 2 inches. For the Mornay sauce, make a cup of thick cream sauce adding ⅓ cup of grated Gruyère or Parmesan cheese. When the puffs have thoroughly cooled, fill each carefully with Mornay sauce. At the moment of serving, put 3 on top of each plate of soup. Do not let them stand in the soup. *Makes 18 or more*

Fish or Shrimp Mousselines

½ **pound fresh shrimp or fish fillets**
1 **cup heavy cream reduced to ½ cup**
Salt and freshly ground pepper

¼ **teaspoon freshly ground nutmeg**
1 **egg white**
Water or broth

When buying shrimp get ½ pound plus 2 shrimps to make up for the weight of the shells. Medium sized shrimp are best for this. Reduce the cream by boiling it 16 minutes, then refrigerating it uncovered until it becomes thick. It is best to do this the day before. Grind the shrimp or fish fillets, using the finest blade of the grinder. Season with salt, pepper, and freshly ground nutmeg. Whisk in the unbeaten egg white and chill the mixture. Beat in the reduced cream and chill several hours.

Make the mousselines in small rounds, using 2 teaspoons to mold them. Scrape them into simmering salted water or broth and cook 3 minutes, covered. The liquid should never boil. Serve 3 or 4 in each plate of chicken or fish soup. *Makes 12 to 16, but the recipe may easily be doubled*

Ricotta Balls for Soup

½ cup ground raw spinach
½ cup ricotta or creamed cottage
   cheese, sieved
1 tablespoon grated Parmesan
   cheese
Salt and pepper
Grated rind of 1 lemon

½ teaspoon nutmeg
1 large egg yolk
¼ cup sifted flour
Flour and grated Parmesan cheese,
   mixed
Consommé

Grind the spinach and press out the juice against a sieve. There should be a little over ⅓ cup of dry spinach. Mix all the ingredients together. Make a small ball, roll it in the mixture of flour and cheese and boil it in consommé to see if it holds together. If not, add 1 or 2 scant tablespoons of flour; the less flour the more delicate the balls are. Simmer them gently in consommé 3 minutes just before serving. Serve 4 or 5 in each cup of soup. *Makes 20 balls*

Royals

⅔ cup cream
2 egg yolks
1 whole egg

Salt and pepper
⅛ teaspoon nutmeg

Scald the cream. Beat the egg yolks and the whole egg together and combine with the cream. Add the seasonings. Pour into an oiled pan so the mixture is ½-inch thick. Bake 12 minutes at 350°. Let cool. Cut it in small cubes to garnish clear soups. The mixture may be baked in tiny fancy oiled molds set in a pan, for 8 to 10 minutes.

Tomato Royals

1 egg	Salt and pepper
2 egg yolks	½ teaspoon fennel powder or
⅓ cup heavy cream	oregano
⅓ cup tomato juice	

Beat the egg and yolks. Mix the cream and juice together, scald, and whisk into the eggs. Add the seasonings and bake according to the directions for Royals.

Sauce Soubise

12 white onions, very thinly sliced	Salt and pepper
¼ cup sweet butter	⅛ teaspoon nutmeg
1 tablespoon flour	1 cup heavy cream
¼ cup hot chicken stock	2 tablespoons sweet butter
2 tablespoons flour	

Soften the onions in the ¼ cup sweet butter in a heavy pot (do not let burn). Stir in 1 tablespoon of flour and when mixture is smooth add the hot stock. Simmer over very low heat 5 minutes, then purée in a blender. Mix the 2 tablespoons flour, the seasonings, and the cream until smooth and add to the purée. Put the purée in the top of a double boiler and cook over simmering water 25 minutes. At the moment of serving stir in the 2 tablespoons sweet butter. This is usually used for gratinées or boiled meat or fish. In Raymond Oliver's *La Soupe aux Huitres* (see index) the sauce must be thicker, so add 3 tablespoons flour instead of 2 the second time.

Vinaigrette Sauce

Vinaigrette sauce is simply French dressing with additions. A pinch of sugar may be added. A wine vinegar is usually used.

BASIC FRENCH DRESSING	ADDITIONS
2 tablespoons vinegar or lemon juice	1 teaspoon Dijon mustard
6 tablespoons olive oil	2 tablespoons minced shallots
Salt and freshly ground pepper	2 tablespoons finely minced fresh herbs, or 2 teaspoons powdered dried herbs

Mix all ingredients together and serve when a piquant sauce is required.

Mayonnaise

2 fresh egg yolks	1½ cups olive oil
¾ teaspoon salt	Vinegar or lemon juice to taste
1 tablespoon wine vinegar	1½ tablespoons boiling water
Freshly ground pepper	¼ teaspoon mustard (optional)

Have all the ingredients at room temperature. The eggs must be left out of the refrigerator 2 hours. Put the egg yolks, salt, vinegar, pepper, and 1 teaspoon oil in mixing bowl and whisk them together until they are thick. Add the rest of the oil drop by drop whisking continuously, until the mixture begins to thicken. I find a good way of adding the oil is to let a ¼ teaspoon of oil drip down the bowl from the rim. After the mayonnaise begins to thicken, the oil may be added slightly faster, and when it is very thick add by tablespoonfuls. If it separates at the beginning, start again with another egg yolk and add the separated mixture drop by drop and it will thicken. Season to taste with a little vinegar or lemon juice. Add the boiling water to make it light and creamy. Mustard may be added at the end if desired.

Sauce Gribiche

2 hard-cooked eggs	2 tablespoons capers
1 cup mayonnaise (see index)	2 tablespoons minced shallots
1 tablespoon minced sour pickles	1 tablespoon Dijon mustard

Mash the egg yolks with a little of the mayonnaise and dice the whites. Mix all the ingredients together. Serve with tête de veau (see index for Soupe à Tête de Veau)

Versions of Crème Fraiche

Crème fraiche in France is so heavy it will hardly pour. It has a slight tang, not quite like our commercial sour cream. I have three versions that are satisfactory.

1. Cream Reduction. Boil 1 cup heavy cream 16 minutes to reduce it to ½ cup very heavy cream. Refrigerate uncovered several hours until it becomes heavy. I usually reduce it the day before I need to use it.

2. Mix half sour cream, half heavy cream together in the required amounts. This may be cooked or used instead of whipped cream.

3. Use 3 ounces cream cheese softened at room temperature, ⅓ to ½ cup sour cream, and 1 cup heavy cream. Whisk the three ingredients

together. The mixture may be spooned out of an earthenware jar at the table. Use over fruit, pastry, etc. This has far more character than ordinary whipped cream.

Other Garnishes

Tiny balls of cooked vegetables
Julienne-stick carrots or other vegetables raw or cooked
Cooked asparagus tips
Melon balls
Avocado balls
Minced fresh herbs
Minced chives and parsley
Small crêpes or omelettes cut in strips
Eggs: soft poached eggs, soft poached egg yolks, sieved or sliced
     hard-cooked eggs
Tiny browned cocktail sausages
Sliced cooked knackwurst or sausages
Button mushrooms or sliced mushrooms
Cooked chestnuts or chestnuts canned in syrup
Truffle sticks marinated in Madeira
Cooked pasta
Grated cheese or diced cheese
Sour cream
Croutons fried in butter with crushed garlic or fennel powder
Canapés of fried bread
Lemon slices dipped in ground parsley

Thickeners

Minute tapioca
Boiled rice
Vermicelli
Pearl barley
Flour
Rice starch
Cornstarch
Arrowroot
Puréeing
Beaten egg yolks
Scalded heavy cream and egg yolks

Index